Fly-Fishing Secrets
of Alaska's Best Guides

Fly-Fishing Secrets of Alaska's Best Guides

WILL RICE

STACKPOLE
BOOKS

Copyright © 2006 by Wilson Rice

Published by
STACKPOLE BOOKS
5067 Ritter Road
Mechanicsburg, PA 17055
www.stackpolebooks.com

Printed in the United States

10 9 8 7 6 5 4 3 2 1

First edition

Photographs by Will Rice
Maps by Martha Tyzenhouse
Cover design by Caroline Stover

Library of Congress Cataloging-in-Publication Data

Rice, Will (Wilson)
    Fly-fishing secrets of Alaska's best guides / Will Rice.— 1st ed.
    p. cm.
    Includes index.
    ISBN-13: 978-0-8117-3313-7
    ISBN-10: 0-8117-3313-0
    1. Fly fishing—Alaska. I. Title.

SH456.R553 2006
799.1'2—dc22
                                    2006006067

Contents

Introduction vii

**PART I: BRISTOL BAY AND SOUTHWEST ALASKA:
         THE STUFF OF DREAMS** 1

1. Rivers of Legend: The Trout Streams of Bristol Bay 3

2. Chasing Rainbows with Jack Holman 9

3. Big Rivers, Big Fish 18

4. Fishing the Big Rivers of Bristol Bay
   with Nanci Morris Lyon 27

5. Southwest Alaska 36

6. Floating Rivers with Chuck Ash 42

**PART II: SOUTH-CENTRAL ALASKA:
         FISHING ALONG THE ROAD SYSTEM** 55

7. The Kenai River System 57

8. Trout Fishing on the Kenai with Bruce Nelson 66

9. Salmon Secrets: A Day on the Kenai
   with Curt Trout and Billy Coulliette 73

10. Susitna Valley 81

11. On the Talkeetna with Chad Valentine 87

**PART III: FISHING THE SALT:
          KODIAK AND RESURRECTION BAY** 95

12. Kodiak Island 97

13. Fly-Fishing Kodiak with Dan Busch 104

14. Salt Water: Fly Rods and Deep Water 111

15. Fishing the Near Shore with Keith Graham
     and Capt. Greg Mercer 115

**PART IV: SOUTHEAST ALASKA
           AND THE LOST COAST** **123**

16. Yakutat and the Lost Coast 125

17. Taking Cohos on the Surface with George Davis 129

18. Southeast Alaska 136

19. Fishing the Rain Forest with Luke Woodruff 141

**PART V: TROPHIES AND TROUBLES:
           ENSURING A SUCCESSFUL TRIP** **147**

20. Landing Big Fish:
     The Techniques of Nanci Morris Lyon 149

21. Bears, Bugs, and Bad Weather 154

22. The Fly Box 165

     Index 179

Introduction

Alaska is a large and complicated place. If you overlaid it on a map of the Lower Forty-eight, you would find that the southeast tip touches Florida, the northernmost point reaches Minnesota, and the Aleutians stretch to the California coast. But size is not its only measure. From rain forest to tundra, oceans to mountains, Alaska is a place of incredible diversity, and that diversity is reflected in the variety of its fisheries. Here a fly fisher may cast dry flies to grayling, swing big leeches for steelhead, or strip heavy baitfish patterns in the open ocean for salmon.

In the thirty years that I have lived—and fished—in Alaska, I have had an opportunity to sample many of the state's fisheries. And every time I fish a new river, there is a steep learning curve. Sometimes I have a guide or an experienced angler to show me the most effective techniques. More often, it is a matter of trial and error, asking questions, and picking up whatever information is available. Over the years, a few how-to books have appeared on the shelves, and they certainly help whenever I explore new water. But the books are invariably divided by species, and the methods that are effective on one stream don't necessarily work in another part of the state, where the conditions are sometimes much different. In Alaska, as everywhere else, local knowledge is the key. And no one has a store of local knowledge like the guides that have fished their home waters for years.

This book is an attempt to gather that local knowledge and, whether you're a newcomer or an old hand, provide you with the kind of information that will ensure you the quality of fishing that you expect from Alaska. That means choosing the type of fishing that appeals to you, having the proper gear and flies, and knowing the basic techniques that are effective on your chosen water. The book won't teach you how to get a good dead drift, but it will explain where, when, and why to use it.

Although the state is large and diverse, the differences in the fisheries are not always geographic. The same techniques that work for fishing the salt water near Seward will work in Kodiak or Southeast. But fishing for trout in the small headwater streams of Bristol Bay is completely different from fishing the larger outlet rivers a few miles away. I decided to organize the book by the major fisheries—sometimes geographic, sometimes by species. Since the same techniques work in various places, the book is cross-referenced to ensure that there is information applicable to almost every fishery, whether I have specifically written about it or not. For instance, the Russian River is a popular trout stream near Anchorage with an ecosystem that is based on its large run of sockeyes. Jack Holman's discussion of fishing similar rivers in Bristol Bay is all you need to know to fish for trout on the Russian.

When I set out to write this book, I wanted to provide information that was as accurate and comprehensive as possible. That meant finding the most skilled and experienced guides in each chosen area. Naming any guide as the best on a given river is both subjective and controversial. The first criterion, obviously, was fishing expertise. But I also wanted to work with those guides who were well respected by their peers and their clients, held themselves to the highest ethical standards, and had as many years of experience as their fisheries allowed. Others may quibble, but every guide who appears in this book was my first choice for his or her particular region.

I wasn't sure what the response would be when I asked them if they were willing to pass along the secrets that they had spent years developing, but I was gratified to discover how generous with their time and expertise all of them turned out to be. Whenever possible, I spent a day or two fishing with the guides (research is always more fun than writing) while they explained the timing, gear, and techniques that are the keys to their success. Being on the water with them gave me better insight into their approach and frequently prompted questions or provided information that I had not previously considered.

Some of these trips were new experiences, and I learned a lot. Even on waters that I have fished for years, they invariably taught me some new twists that dramatically improved my fishing. I hope you will learn as much from reading this book as I learned from writing it.

I expected to find a certain consistency to the approaches taken under similar circumstances, and to a certain extent that proved true. After all, cohos act the same in southeast Alaska as they do in Bristol Bay. Generally, the techniques used by the various guides under identical conditions are similar, regardless of the specific geographic location. But I was surprised at the amount of dissimilar, and sometimes contradictory, advice I received. If consistency is the hobgoblin of small minds, then I have avoided the problem here. I have made no attempt to reconcile differing opinions or techniques. They are simply proof that there is no single best way to catch any fish. If one guide's technique doesn't work on a given day, try someone else's.

One note on species identification. Alaskan salmon all have two names, and they are often used interchangeably. To the frustration of my editor, I have adopted that same approach. Chinooks and kings are the same fish, as are cohos and silvers, and sockeyes and reds. Dolly Varden and arctic char are different species, but only a biologist can tell the difference, and I have made no attempt to distinguish them.

I particularly want to express my appreciation to each of the guides included in this book. Without exception, they were gracious, knowledgeable, and a lot of fun to fish with. They and their staffs went far beyond my expectations in making this book possible. I wholeheartedly recommend any of them if you're hoping to realize your Alaskan dreams.

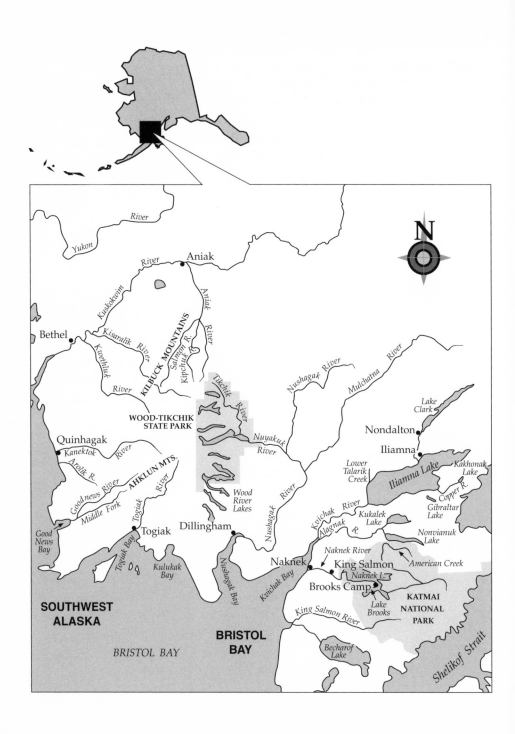

PART I

BRISTOL BAY AND SOUTHWEST ALASKA: THE STUFF OF DREAMS

When a fly fisher imagines Alaska, this area is invariably the site of his dreams. It stretches in a long curve from the Alaska Peninsula in the south past the mouth of the Kuskokwim to the west. It hosts massive runs of salmon and includes the westernmost range of rainbow trout in North America.

This is almost entirely wilderness, and access to the fishing is by floatplane, boat, or a combination of the two. The rivers provide fly-rod fishing for all five species of salmon and have the best rainbow and char fishing in the state. Bears are a constant on many of the rivers. Fishing these waters can be spectacular, but it is never cheap. If you are looking for the ultimate Alaskan fly-fishing trip and you have the money to spend, this is the place to start.

The best known of these fisheries are the small, clear spawning streams of Bristol Bay, where rainbows and char grow fat on salmon eggs and carcasses. Jack Holman and his sons have fished these rivers for years. The flies and techniques that they have developed will work on any of the small upper-system streams where you find rainbows and spawning sockeyes. Jack also explains what to look for in selecting a fly-out lodge.

The biggest trout in Alaska come from the biggest rivers. Nanci Morris Lyon will tell you how to make that dream of a thirty-incher come true. Although she focuses on the big three of Bristol Bay, those same methods work on any large river.

For the angler who wants to see the real Alaska, absent of people and airplanes, few opportunities can match a week spent floating a river in southwest Alaska. Chuck Ash has shown these rivers to a number of lucky anglers. His territory may be remote, but the methods he uses for trout, kings, and cohos are applicable to any medium-size, clear-water river in the state. Some of his techniques require a higher skill level than those used by other guides, but the rewards are commensurate with the effort. Chuck also tells you the questions to ask if you are planning a multiday guided float trip.

1

RIVERS OF LEGEND:
The Trout Streams of Bristol Bay

We all have the same vision of Alaskan fishing: floatplanes overhead, grizzly bears ambling along tundra ridges, and clear riffling rivers flush with spawning sockeyes and feeding rainbows. In spite of its iconic stature, it is an image rooted almost exclusively in a handful of streams found in the upper corner of Bristol Bay. Their names resonate among fly fishers the world over—Brooks River, Moraine Creek, Lower Talarik Creek, Kulik, Idavain, Copper River, Gibraltar, Little Ku, Battle Creek. And these rivers deserve their reputation.

Most originate among the granite peaks of the Aleutian Range and fall within the protection of Katmai National Park. The high, rocky country gives them an unforgettable beauty, whether it is the sharp spires that surround the upper stretches of American Creek or the spruce forest lining the Copper River. All of these streams lie far from the nearest town or road. There are lodges on two of the rivers, Brooks and Kulik, but even those are accessible only by floatplane. Even the most remote creeks are no longer the secrets they once were, and the Beavers and Cessnas arrive early from area lodges. The solitude may be gone, but the fishing is as good as ever.

The streams are all of a type—thirty to fifty yards wide, moderate flow, thigh-deep and wadable. The occasional boulder field punctuates classic salmon spawning beds—geologic remnants of the last ice age. Willows and alders flourish on the banks, and gravel bars line the inside bends. Some of them, like Moraine and American Creeks, begin high above treeline and tumble, riffle and run, through rolling tundra.

Others are lined with forests of spruce and birch. These are rivers that seem designed for fly fishing, and most of them are managed as fly-fishing only, catch-and-release waters.

A couple of these rivers, American and Moraine, can be rafted by the adventurous, and there are a few opportunities to camp alongside others. Given the large numbers of bears that frequent all of these rivers, however, camping is best left to those with lots of Alaskan experience—and even they often suffer from trashed camps and destroyed gear. With the exception of Brooks River, almost all of the fishing pressure is lodge based and guided. Those daily fly-outs don't come cheap, but that is a problem common to all of the world's premier wilderness fisheries.

There is a common thread that makes these specific rivers among the world's greatest trout streams: Each of them is a tributary to a lake large enough to act as a nursery for the millions of sockeye salmon fry that hatch every May. Sockeyes are the engine that powers the entire Bristol Bay ecosystem. Every summer, their bodies transport thousands of tons of nutrients from the plankton-rich ocean depths to the upland waters of their natal streams. They provide food for their own young, eagles, bears, and most important for our purposes, rainbow trout. The life cycle of the sockeye lies at the heart of what many people consider the finest cold-water fishery in North America. And understanding the nuances of that life cycle is the key to knowing how to catch the trout and char that depend on the salmon.

Rainbows begin their own spawning migration from the lakes to the rivers in April as the ice begins to break up and the water to warm. Slow and emaciated from winter's hardships, they are greeted by the first reliable food source of the year. Salmon eggs, which have lain in the gravel beds over the winter, begin to hatch. Tiny alevins, less than an inch long and still absorbing the yolk sac, wriggle through the interstices in the gravel and emerge along the river bottom. They are completely vulnerable, their only defense their overwhelming numbers. Although they are a major food source, and there are some wonderful imitative flies, they are of little importance to the angler. The season is closed to protect the spawning trout.

By June 8, when the season traditionally opens, the alevins have grown into inch-long, free-swimming fry. Hatched in flowing water, the fry will spend the first year of life along the edges of lakes that lie downstream. Moving largely in the dim light of dusk and dawn, the fry migrate past the pods of hungry trout and char. Slashing strikes and swirling boils mark their passage. Arctic terns cut and weave through the air, picking off the tiny fry from above. Even grayling, the ultimate insectivores, gorge on the bounty. If the snowmelt cooperates and the rivers don't blow out, it can be a brief but exciting fishery.

Many fishers mistakenly refer to the phenomenon as a smolt run. It is not, although both occur at the same time. Smolt are year-old fish, three or four inches long, that have wintered over in the lakes and are now outmigrating to the ocean. They occur only in those rivers that drain a lake. A few of the rivers we are discussing here, such as Kulik and Brooks, lie between lakes and thus may hold both fry and smolt. But those who wish to fish a true smolt migration should look to the large outlet rivers, such as the Naknek and Kvichak (pronounced kwee-jack).

Tiny, inch-long streamers are the patterns of choice in June. But fry imitations are not the only flies that work in the early season. Alaskan rainbows seem to love nothing better than marabou or a strip of rabbit fur writhing in the current, and bunny leeches, sculpin patterns, and Woolly Buggers are always effective. The real highlight of early fishing, though, is the occasional warm, sunny day when the trout are looking up and willing to hit dry flies. You won't find the kind of hatches here that are prevalent on most trout waters, but these fish are hungry and omnivorous at this time of year, and the topwater action can be spectacular.

By about June 20, the sockeyes—which Alaskans usually call red salmon, or simply reds—begin to flood into these rivers, pushing the trout out of position. They are sleek and silver when they leave the ocean, hard fighting and single-mindedly obsessed with reaching the spawning grounds. Nose to tail, four and five abreast, they move upstream in a seemingly unbroken string that goes on for days. Some spawn in the lakes themselves or in the larger rivers flowing out of them, but most move into the upper tributaries. Leaping fish and swirling wakes from the milling schools mark their arrival at the mouths of the spawning streams.

The same internal calendar that brings the sockeyes back on a predictable date seems to work for the bears. Invariably, with the arrival of the first salmon come the first bears, usually sows with cubs and young

bears on their own for the first time. They wander the rivers, hoping
for an early meal, but healthy fish are difficult to catch. The remaining
bears, including the big boars, move in within a few weeks, taking up
their station in the best fishing holes, where rapids or waterfalls concentrate the migrating fish. In some places, like Brooks River, both the
bears and the bear-watchers outnumber the anglers.

The number of fishers on these streams has largely habituated the
bears to their presence, but that doesn't mean the bears should be taken
lightly. Regardless of the casual indifference that most of them display,
there is always the possibility of a problem with young bears just on
their own, old boars, sows with cubs, or any bear on a kill. Everyone
venturing into this country should have a basic understanding of
proper bear etiquette.

Trout fishing takes a backseat during July. The massive schools of
sockeyes push the rainbows and char into less obvious lies, where they
are difficult to find. Good trout fishing is still available, but most anglers
who head for Bristol Bay in July are targeting salmon. Even these
upper rivers hold freshly arrived fish that are still bright and solid.

Sockeyes, like all salmon, quit feeding when they hit fresh water.
Unlike their piscivorous cousins, however, they feed on krill and plankton during their years in the ocean. Consequently, they do not possess
even the vestigial search image that makes king and coho salmon
aggressive. In many streams, it is almost impossible to persuade a fresh
sockeye to hit a fly. Most of the fish that are caught have been inadver-
tently, or deliberately, snagged in the mouth when the leader swings
through the school, dragging the fly behind. In a few rivers, however,
sockeyes seem willing to mouth a fly presented at exactly their level.
Although large, brightly colored bucktails, often called Russian River
or coho flies, are common, most serious salmon fishers use small, sparse
patterns.

Once in the spawning streams, the salmon begin to darken up and
lose their desirability as sport fish. They move into the slower pools and
eddies in the rivers, holding in vast schools as their bodies ripen for
their penultimate contribution to the ecosystem. By August, the
salmon have transformed into Halloween caricatures with scarlet bodies, deep green heads, and in the males, hooked jaws snaggled with jutting teeth. The fights among the males are vicious, while the females
wear down their tails digging spawning redds in the gravel. Ironically,

now that they are no longer a suitable sport fish, the males will attack any fly, making the trout fishing frustrating.

As the sockeyes pair up, the scent of ripening eggs attracts the rainbows and char. They begin to stack up at the tailouts of the spawning runs, risking the wrath of the aggressive male salmon as they make forays into the danger zone. The redd-building activity of the females stirs up the insect life hidden in the gravel, and although the trout are looking for eggs, they will readily hit a well-drifted nymph.

Once the spawning starts, the trout move into position immediately behind the now-focused salmon, fattening up on the protein-rich diet of loose eggs. Spawning has a frantic choreography of its own, with each pair of salmon racing to complete the dance before their bodies are self-consumed. This is the peak fishing of the season, with even the largest trout moving up out of the lakes to feed. In a gravel riffle speckled with the scarlet bodies of spawning salmon, the dark olive backs of the rainbows stand out. But for every dark-bodied bow, there are usually several bright lake fish that are far more difficult to see. Char are even better camouflaged, giving themselves away only by the white leading edges of their fins.

In spite of the abundance of food and the substantial numbers of fish, there are times when the August fishing is frustratingly difficult. The fish see so many natural eggs that they become very selective to size and color. Drifts must be drag-free, except when fishing for char, which sometimes relish an egg hanging in the current. The most difficult problem, however, is not in getting strikes, but in detecting them. The trout become adept at spitting out anything that does not feel and taste like the real thing. Almost all fishing is done with a strike indicator, and a skilled nymph fisher has a distinct advantage.

In recent years, the guides solved the problem of missed strikes by putting a bead of the appropriate size and color a couple inches above a bare hook and pinning it in place with a piece of toothpick. Pegged beads, as they are known, make it impossible for a trout to spit out the imitation without getting snagged by the trailing hook. Highly controversial, beads are so effective that their use has become ubiquitous among the lodges, even in fly-fishing-only water. For those anglers who would prefer to use traditional fly-fishing techniques, read the interview with Chuck Ash, who still believes that fly fishing means fishing with flies.

The peak of the spawn brings a bounty to the wildlife. Bears wander the river like teenagers in a buffet line. Gulls line the banks, so gorged that they can barely fly. The trout pick their way through a conveyor belt of eggs washing down from the redds. Dying even as they spawn, the salmon, which have not fed since they left salt water, have absorbed so much of their own fat that in the end, the bears and gulls focus on the eggs, eyes, and brains—the only things left of the salmon with any nutrients. The carcasses remain for a last gorging by the trout and finally as fertilizer for the plankton that will sustain their own young the following summer. Within a few short weeks it ends, but the trout continue to feed voraciously on the salmon carcasses.

With the trout fattening up for the winter, fishing remains good even after the salmon have spawned and died. Flesh flies are the usual fly of choice, but sculpin patterns and big leeches are equally effective. Late season often brings the biggest fish of the year.

As the food dwindles, the trout drop back downstream into the lakes. An autumn rain heavy enough to wash out the carcasses will empty a river of trout within a few days. Few people see them leave, though. By October, the Bristol Bay weather, and its effect on flying, has driven the few remaining fishers to the Naknek and Kvichak, rivers that can be best fished by boat.

The season is short on these streams, a scant four months, but compressing the life cycle of millions of salmon into that period creates an intensity in everything connected with it, including the fishing. There is little wonder that these few rivers epitomize Alaskan fishing.

It is not only the rivers of Bristol Bay that are legendary. So are the guides. Early lodge owners like Chris Goll, Bill Sims, and Ted Gerken not only pioneered this fishery, but also helped ensure its health and longevity. They belong to a generation that is rapidly diminishing, but their children and protégés remain.

One of the finest of that generation of guides is Jack Holman, who has owned and operated No-See-Um Lodge for almost thirty years. His sons and their families share much of the work, but Jack still flies one of the lodge's immaculate Beavers and continues to introduce new groups of fly fishers to the country in which he has spent most of his life. Few people are more suited to teach a master's class in fly-fishing Bristol Bay than Jack Holman and his sons John and Matt.

2

CHASING RAINBOWS
with Jack Holman

For trout fishers throughout the world, the rivers of Bristol Bay are a lifetime dream. Many consider it to be the best rainbow trout fishing in North America, and the stunning wilderness setting heightens its allure. Gravel-bottomed streams, alive with spawning sockeye, flow through verdant tundra hills. Rainbows that average two to four pounds, and grow much larger, hang like shadows behind the scarlet-backed salmon, fattening themselves for a dark and brutal winter. These are streams that can be reached only by floatplane, and for most people, that means staying at a fly-out lodge.

Guiding is a competitive game, and few judges are more harsh than a guide's peers. However, you would be hard-pressed to find any lodge owner more universally respected by his competition than Jack Holman, the owner of No-See-Um Lodge on the Kvichak. Early every morning during the season, Jack climbs into his immaculate red-and-white DeHavilland Beaver and takes clients to rivers that he has been fishing for more than thirty years. It is a heritage he has passed on to his sons. John and Matt both work as pilot-guides for the lodge and are well on their way to surpassing even their father in their knowledge of fly-fishing the legendary streams of the area.

I have had several opportunities to fish with Jack and his sons and have always come away with a sense of how much I have yet to learn about catching trout in Alaska. On the final day of my last visit, they put me onto more big Dollies than could be counted, and I managed, on successive casts, to take a twenty-four- and a twenty-three-inch rainbow on dry flies. That evening, sitting around the crew quarters with Jack, John, Matt, and one of their chief guides, Jeff Parker, I got an opportunity to pick their brains on how to fish the spawning rivers of the area, information that carries over to any small trout stream with a run of sockeye salmon.

Trout season in Bristol Bay begins on June 8 every year, and the fishing can be superb. The salmon fry have emerged from the streambed gravel and are beginning to migrate downstream to the lakes where they will spend the first year of their lives. The trout gorge on them. Everyone knows what the fish are feeding on, but in spite of this, Jack says that fry are the most difficult trout food to consistently imitate successfully. I was happy to hear that, because after twenty years of fishing these streams during mid-June, I have never found the perfect fly. John's comment about the myriad of different fry patterns is that they all work some of the time, but none of them works all of the time. Nevertheless, the rigs and flies that they used were the most effective that I have seen.

During the fry outmigration, a lot of slashing surface activity takes place, with the trout actively chasing the fleeing fry. Flies that float high in the water column, like Thunder Creeks, are common imitations and have been my mainstay for years. But on American Creek, Jack's son Matt showed me a far more effective rig. He had me fishing deep, dead drifting a realistic pattern under a strike indicator. He suggested using enough weight to just tick the bottom, which will orient the fly with its head upstream. The strike indicator was positioned fairly high on the leader, an indication of the depth of water that the trout and char prefer. In those streams where it is legal, a flashy nymph or fry imitation fished as a dropper under a dry fly also works well.

No-See-Um guides like epoxy-headed flies with a bit of marabou or similar material to give some motion to the tail. Some of the patterns look as if they could swim out of your hand, but the variety of flies the guides carry makes it clear that there is no one secret pattern. Whether you are fishing on the surface or deep, fry patterns are always fished on a floating line.

Articulated Leeches, Egg-Sucking Leeches, and Bunny Flies are early-season standbys in all of the streams. These rivers have large sculpin populations, so Woolhead Sculpins and similar patterns fished along the bottom will take some of the biggest trout in the river. In the larger rivers, they are best fished with a sinking-tip line, but a floater will work if the runs are not too deep and fast.

Alaska trout have long had a reputation as feeding only on eggs, flesh, and smolt. But much more insect activity takes place than most anglers realize, particularly during the first half of the season. The common wisdom is that the trout fishing goes dead from late June through July. In fact, this is the time when all those traditional fly-fishing techniques come into play. Jack and his guides have spent a lot of time developing the nymph and dry-fly fishing on these streams, and when the fishing is on, it is as good as you can find anywhere.

Dry flies are the most fun to fish. It is unusual to see the steady feeding behavior that you will find on a spring creek, but that doesn't mean that the fish won't hit a surface pattern. If you see any rising fish, the chances are good that a dry fly will fool them. The fish don't usually see hatches heavy enough to become selective (although it can happen, and you had better have some variety in your fly box when it does). However, there are times when they will hit a big attractor and other times when they want something smaller and more realistic.

Jack's favorite patterns are Green Drake imitations. By late June, the big bugs start coming off, particularly on overcast, drizzly days. The hatch extends through the end of July and at times can be very heavy. Few things in the world will get big trout—and we are talking two-footers here—looking up like a green drake hatch does. Jack likes the larger, extended-body imitations, but any big Wulff, Humpy, or similar fly will fool the fish.

The predominant hatches in Alaska are caddis. They can be found on most streams all summer, and although they don't usually result in steadily feeding trout, they keep the fish interested. Jack likes Stimulators, in yellow or tan, and Elk Hair Caddis in sizes 14 and 16. Caddis imitations can be dead drifted or skated, and char in particular will hit a skated fly.

Some streams have a population of large (size 8) black stoneflies. They crawl out on logs to hatch, and the larval cases are a sure tip-off that bugs are moving. Try a big Stonefly Nymph or Prince Nymph if you want to go deep. Sofa Pillows, Bugmeisters, Stimulators, and similar patterns work well if any stones are hatching and make great attractor patterns when there is no hatch.

It is only within the last few years that fly fishers have figured out that nymphs are as deadly here as in the Lower Forty-eight. When I asked the guys about nymph patterns, they all just said "beadheads." Weight and flash are important, and beadheads fit the bill. The specific patterns that they use include Copper Johns, Bird's Nests, Prince Nymphs, and Flashback Pheasant Tails. Most of the nymphs are tied in sizes 14 to 18, but they carry some rubber-leg stonefly nymphs in sizes 10 to 12. Jeff Parker, an old Lee's Ferry guide, went back to his roots and tried midge patterns with surprising success, particularly on difficult trout. He likes Zebra Midges in size 16.

The critical thing with nymphs is always the drift. Jack says that he likes to use as little weight as necessary to get the fly down to the bottom. In some cases it's important to get the fly deep quickly, and more weight is required, but for the most part a pure dead drift is ideal. Poly yarn indicators work the best, and Jack likes to use white, which the trout seem to ignore. On those bright, overcast days when the water turns to a pewter sheen, a black indicator is much easier to see. Matt says that he carries a black marker in his kit to color a portion of the indicator. The contrast between black and white makes the yarn particularly easy to follow. When you are fishing in an area where every splashing salmon has you looking around for a bear, it's important to have an indicator that you can spot quickly. If the wind is blowing too hard for yarn indicators, corkies are easier to cast.

For years, fishing writers have said that the returning schools of sockeyes push the trout out of the rivers during July, making the fishing very poor. Although that is true in some rivers, particularly the larger ones like the Naknek and Kvichak, substantial numbers of trout remain in the smaller salmon spawning streams. In fact, a close look at the pods of migrating sockeyes will often reveal a salmon-size trout accompanying them. The salmon do move the trout from their preferred lies, however. Look for fish in shallow riffles, deep fast chutes, along the cut banks and edges, and in the back eddies—all places that the salmon avoid. Jack says that on occasion he sees pods of trout, a dozen or more, packed tightly together up under a cut bank—apparently a defense against the aggressive male salmon. They are not feeding when they are holding like this, though, so there is little point in trying to tempt them.

The same techniques that work early in the season will catch trout in July. Leeches, nymphs, and dry flies are the usual patterns, but if a lot of bears are on the river, and they are ripping up the salmon, try eggs and flesh flies. Some of the best fish of the summer are caught this way.

Once the salmon pair up and begin building their redds, the trout will move in behind them looking for food. Although there are no eggs in the water at this point, the nest building stirs up the bottom gravel and flushes nymphs into the water. This is a great time to sight-fish nymphs to the waiting trout. At times, though, the number of salmon digging in the bottom will turn the water so dirty that it is unfishable.

The timing of the sockeye spawning varies from river to river. Generally speaking, the spawning begins earliest in the highest streams. Salmon in rivers closer to sea level, like Brooks, may not spawn until September.

Once spawning begins in earnest, Jack and his guides switch exclusively to beads. They peg them two inches above the hook or, in fly-fishing-only water, above a simple fly. They use a yarn indicator and enough weight to get the fly down but not so much as to make it hang up on the bottom. A dead drift is essential. In heavily fished rivers, they may use no weight at all, because the trout have become conditioned, by being hooked, to eating eggs that are upwelling in the current. Split shot are usually attached twelve to eighteen inches above the hook.

The color of the bead is very important, and No-See-Um guides carry up to forty different colors—changing them until they find the one the fish want on that particular day. John pointed out to me that the eggs are never a single color and that if you want to match the natural, you have to look at the eggs underwater, where the colors of the beads and eggs differ slightly from their colors in the air.

Once the spawning is over, flesh flies come into their own. Big Articulated Leeches in white and salmon pink work well. The fish will still eat eggs as well, which have the advantage of being fished on a floating line. Mice and dark-colored leeches are also productive at this time of year. The trout are fattening up for the winter fast and are usually eager to hit a chunky fly.

Although the fishing can remain good fairly late in the year, the trout will move out of these upper streams almost overnight. A heavy fall rain that washes the carcasses out will also empty the river of trout.

I asked Jack about the skills needed to fish these waters, and there was no hesitation in his answer: "A good drag-free drift is the most critical element of our fishing. Distance casting isn't very useful on these small waters. It's much more important to be able to make a short, accurate cast. The most common mistake I see people make is trying to cast too far. We're not casting, we're fishing."

A willingness to listen to the guide is also important. Although many techniques from other areas, both in and out of Alaska, have some carry-over benefits, these streams are different enough that local knowledge makes a distinct difference. Jack says that often an experienced fisherman brings along a wife who has never fished. "We can usually have her outfishing him within three days, because she will do what we tell her, but he won't listen."

Everyone who fishes these rivers is aware of the bears. Jack says that they usually see bears every day. Bears are the most difficult in June, when they are ravenously hungry but cannot catch the still-fresh salmon that are starting to come into the river. Moose calves are also around at this time, and they are a favorite prey of the big grizzlies. A bear guarding a kill is a very dangerous animal.

Guns are not allowed in Katmai National Park, which is where most of the streams are located. These bears have seen enough anglers that they are habituated—which does not mean tame—so you need to give them respect and as much distance as possible. Bears generally are not interested in confrontations, although the young subadult males will sometimes test their status with people. I have seen John chase off curious bears that approached too closely by throwing rocks in front of them or splashing water at them.

Gear is always an important issue for fishing these streams—not because it's esoteric, but because you'd better have it with you when you're fishing. It's not as if you can walk back to the car and grab a rain jacket when the storm rolls in.

Waders should be Gore-Tex, with felt-soled boots. Cleats are unnecessary and can damage an aircraft's aluminum skin. You'd better leave a really big tip if you damage some pilot's half-million-dollar baby. These rivers are cold, so poly long johns or wading pants under your waders are necessary.

Dress in layers. A hot, sunny morning can turn into driving rain in the afternoon, and an early fog can burn off to T-shirt weather. Never—

let me repeat that—never leave the plane without taking a rain jacket. Fingerless gloves and a stocking cap take up little space and make a dramatic difference in comfort, especially on a boat run. Windstopper jackets have become the outer layer of choice when it isn't raining.

Take two rods. You will want a spare, and different weights make the types of fishing more fun. Jack recommends a 5- and a 7-weight. Lighter rods harm the fish, because you have to tire them out too much before you land them. Spey rods are becoming more common, and although you don't really need the extra distance, the line control ability helps you get good drifts.

You don't need a saltwater-quality drag or capacity, but use a decent reel. A thirty-inch rainbow is the fish of a lifetime, and you don't want your lightweight trout reel freezing up when you hook one. For early season, a floating line and a sinking-tip with a medium sink rate will both be useful. If you are traveling in August, all of the fishing will be with a floating line. Tapered leaders are best for fishing nymphs, drys, and eggs. Jack likes fluorocarbon tippets. Carry spools of 3X, 4X, and 5X.

Other gear you will need includes bug dope (get the serious stuff) and a head net if you find insects to be particularly annoying. Good polarized glasses are critical. You'll be doing a lot of sight fishing, and you need polarized lenses to see the fish. Hemostats or good pliers are also important.

SELECTING A FLY-OUT LODGE

Fly-out lodges may be the ultimate in Alaskan fly fishing, but they are not cookie-cutter copies. You'll find a wide range of offerings, from lodges that have a single plane for a large number of guests to those that provide a plane and pilot all day for a small group. Prices generally reflect the services provided, but anyone paying the kind of money that these places cost should know what to expect going in.

"When selecting a lodge, the number-one question should always be 'What do I do if we can't fly?'" Jack advises. Weather is always a factor in Bristol Bay, and having good home water is the salvation for those days when the fog is down on the deck. Some very good lodges have beautiful locations, remote with spectacular views, but no fishing that is easily accessible by boat. When the weather closes in, it's time to break out the cards or books. Lodges that are located on river systems always have alternative fishing available during weather when the planes can't fly—and bad weather can make for very good fishing.

Almost as important is the number of clients the lodge accommo-dates—or, more specifically, as Jack puts it, the plane-to-guest ratio—which varies substantially. For instance, No-See-Um can host ten guests and has two Beavers and a Cessna 206 exclusively for their use, as well as a Cessna 185 on floats to handle the lodge chores. This means there is a guide for each pair of guests and a plane available at all times. If it turns out that the original destination stream is blown out or not fishing well, the guides can look for alternatives. This is not a minor issue. While I was at the lodge, one group of guests found that the fish-ing at Kulik was unusually poor. They checked Moraine, but wind conditions there would have made fishing difficult, so they flew to Brooks River and found the best dry-fly action of the week.

The more common arrangement is for the plane to drop off the anglers and pick them up at the end of the day. This may not be opti-mum, but it works well on most days. The real problem with this arrangement is not the fishing—even with a plane, not every day will be great—but when the weather unexpectedly changes and the plane can't get in to pick up the passengers. Almost every year, someone ends up stuck in a storm for a night or two. Unless there is a cabin or other shelter around, it can get very uncomfortable and nerve-racking.

Some lodges advertise as fly-outs but do most of their fishing from boats, with a rotating group of guests being flown out each day. This arrangement is cheaper and, as long as you know about it when you book, perfectly acceptable. The big issue here is the type of plane used for the fly-out. If the lodge is operating a large aircraft, such as an Otter, a lot of guests will be squeezed onto a stream that may already have other people on it. These are small streams, and fishing a run with a dozen other people is a far cry from two anglers and a guide.

The amount of experience the pilots and guides have is also important. A steep learning curve exists during the first year for both professions, and there is a marked difference in abilities after that initial season. Many guides and pilots have worked in this area for decades and have the skill and experience to provide as high-quality a trip as conditions will allow. Others have never been to Alaska before they took the job and may be little more than baby-sitters with good cast-ing skills.

Jack also emphasizes that a lodge should make clear just what is included in the price. Some lodges charge extra for fly-outs. Some include transportation from Anchorage rather than King Salmon, a significant difference. When you have a whole day's worth of fishing lies to tell, the cost of drinks also can add up. Some lodges provide flies for their guests. They are always better than the "Alaskan selection" that a fly shop will sell you, but if the lodge is charging you for them, costs can mount.

Alaska has such a fabled reputation and is so different from the Lower Forty-eight that a visitor's expectations may be unrealistic. Occasionally a booking agent will oversell a trip. Guests may believe that every day will be like the five-minute segments on the promotional DVD. As Jack says, "It's still fishing—there are going to be good days and bad days."

Fishing in Alaska is different week by week and year by year. The biggest problem is the weather. Streams wash out. Flights get canceled. Rain, particularly in August, and wind, worst in September, hamper fishing. A good guide knows how to minimize these problems. Lake-fed streams rarely blow out, and tree-lined rivers are easier to fish in the wind than a stream high in the tundra—but not even the best guides can make the fish bite when they have lockjaw.

Having slogged over the tundra with Jack a few times, I wondered whether a client needs to be in top physical shape to fish these streams. Jack says he's had a number of clients who still fished with him into their eighties. You do need a realistic idea of your abilities, however. The right attitude is much more important. Every lodge has options that require little in the way of strength or stamina, but other trips will leave a reasonably fit person in his or her late fifties—that would be me—worn out at the end of the day. The one difficulty is with children. Jack says that his only real problem is with kids who are under thirteen years old, which is just too young to have the self-discipline that these trips require.

Not everyone will get a chance to spend a week flying out to trout-rich rivers, eating gourmet meals, and staying in a wilderness lodge. But if you have the opportunity, it can be the trip of a lifetime. And if you don't, the knowledge that Jack and his sons have acquired over the decades will stand you in good stead on any number of less exotic Alaskan rivers.

3

BIG RIVERS, BIG FISH

We've all seen those photos on the covers of fly-fishing mags—a beaming angler holding a monstrous fat-bellied rainbow—and we've all dreamed of just once in our lives hooking a fish that big. Most of us consider a ten-pound native rainbow caught on a fly in a free-flowing river as no more than a fantasy. But there is one section of the country where you have a good shot at realizing that fantasy. Three rivers in Bristol Bay—the Naknek, Kvichak, and Alagnak—drain the major lakes of the region. Millions of salmon move through those rivers, creating a food source that grows very large predators. These are big rivers with big fish, and they are hallowed waters for those in search of trophy trout.

Much of Bristol Bay's reputation as a trout fishery comes from its smaller streams, such as Brooks and the Copper. These legendary rivers drain the west slopes of the Aleutian Range and provide spawning grounds for Bristol Bay's huge sockeye runs. The result is a huge biomass of eggs, smolt, and flesh that eventually flows into the four major lake systems: Iliamna, Naknek, Nonvianuk, and Kukaklek Lakes. It is the rivers that drain these lakes that we are discussing here: the Kvichak, flowing from Iliamna; the eponymous Naknek; and the Alagnak, whose branches drain Nonvianuk and Kukaklek.

Most of the rainbows that winter in these lakes move into the upper drainages, following the sockeyes. But plenty of fish, including the largest, drop down into the outlet rivers to feed. An abundance of

18

food is available. Kings and chums spawn exclusively in the big rivers. They are joined by a significant number of sockeye, pinks, and cohos. The result is a true trophy fishery.

A "big" trout from the Naknek or Kvichak is usually defined as one that's at least thirty inches, and when the fishing is at its best, in autumn, these fish are fat and heavy. The trout from the Alagnak run a bit smaller but still hit twenty-eight inches or so. In addition to the rainbows, a fly fisher in the right spot at the right time can target king salmon, cohos, sockeyes, chums, pinks, Dolly Varden, and grayling.

Unlike their counterparts in the Lower Forty-eight, Alaskan rainbows are highly migratory. Although they are not steelhead and don't go to sea, they do move in and out of the lakes as the season progresses. Like steelhead, they are broad shouldered and maintain the silvery sheen that acts as camouflage in open water. Only after they have been in the river for a period of time, particularly during spring spawning, do they develop the strong spotting and colors of resident rainbows. Timing is the key to having a shot at big fish, almost as important for these rainbows as it is for salmon. As with almost all trout in Alaska, the lives of these fish follow the rhythms of the salmon spawning cycle, and knowledge of that cycle is as important on these big rivers as it is on the headwater streams.

Sockeyes are the primary component of that cycle in Bristol Bay. Sockeye fry migrate down into the lakes after hatching and spend their first winter there. The following spring, these fish, now smolt that have grown to about two and a half to three inches long, begin to migrate out to sea. The smolt move through the upper water column in big schools, and no angler who has ever intercepted one of those schools will forget it. Terns and gulls dive-bomb them, wheeling and screaming as the fish move downstream. From underneath, the trout slash like bluefish, throwing wakes and leaving stunned and bloodied smolt to be picked up at leisure. The whole show sweeps downstream so fast that it is possible to get only a few casts into the frenzy before it passes.

Like fall-run steelhead, a lot of trout overwinter in the big rivers preparatory to spawning in the early spring. The trout that spent the winter in the lakes drop down to join them as the ice begins to go out. Many of these fish remain in the rivers after spawning to take advantage of the smolt migration, but there is already some movement back to the lakes. Some of the best fishing is found right at the outlets of the lakes, and the June 8 opening of trout season usually sees a pretty good group of anglers working the area where the current is just starting to pick up.

The smolt action is exciting, but most of the early-season trout are taken by dragging big leeches, streamers, and sculpins across the bottom. *Big* is the operative word, too, with some articulated flies stretching four inches long. Anglers usually have a couple weeks of good trout fishing before the sockeyes show up. The nose-to-tail migrating schools initially displace the trout from their favored lies.

By July, the salmon have returned in force. As they begin the morphological transformation into their spawning bodies, the males become more aggressive and territorial, and they push the trout back up into the lakes. The Alagnak and Kvichak have some resident fish that remain in the river all summer, but they tend to be smaller than the trophy trout that show up in the fall. These resident fish are forced into shallow edges, back channels, or deeper water but are still actively feeding. The Naknek, perhaps because only the upper ten miles or so hold trout, sees essentially all of its rainbows migrate upstream into Naknek Lake in July.

When the trout move out of the rivers, the anglers' interest turns to salmon. The salmon runs and their availability to a fly fisher vary from river to river here, but generally speaking, you'll find good king, chum, and coho fishing on the Alagnak; sockeyes and silvers on the Naknek; and chums and silvers on the Kvichak. The massive runs of sockeyes that once moved through the Kvichak system have inexplicably dwindled over the past few years, but there is hope that they will recover in the near future.

By early August, the fishing begins to improve dramatically. The cohos, usually referred to by Alaskans as silvers, start to show up. These are not true destination rivers for cohos, but there are enough fish around to provide some variety for the trout angler. By about mid-August, the trout have begun to move back down out of the lakes, taking up feeding stations behind the spawning salmon. The smaller fish arrive first, and more and more large fish appear as the season wears on. With all five species of salmon spawning, the late summer provides a bounty of eggs and, later, flesh to hungry rainbows. From the first spawning kings right through the late-fall die-off of silvers, the trout are hungry and aggressive. This is the finest fishing of the year and the best chance to hook a real trophy.

Although there are enough similarities among the Naknek, Kvichak, and Alagnak to consider them together, there are also some important differences.

NAKNEK RIVER

Naknek Lake butts up against the Aleutian Range, and its waters have the characteristic aquamarine color that comes from its headwater glaciers. The Naknek River flows out of the lake and empties into Bristol Bay, only twenty-five miles downstream. The river flows past the town of King Salmon, one of the major hubs of Bristol Bay. Handy accommodations and a choice of restaurants make the Naknek perhaps the most convenient river to fish in Bristol Bay.

Other than back-trolling for king salmon in the lower stretches, most of the fishing on the Naknek is concentrated in the uppermost ten miles of river, between the outlet of the lake and a section known as Rapids Camp. At its outlet, the mouth of the lake is broad and shallow, with current almost nonexistent. Shallow depressions mark the current flows and provide that tiny bit of extra cover the trout are looking for. This stretch has good early-season fishing, as the rainbows lie in wait for the waves of smolt that must pass through on their way to the ocean. From the outlet down to Rapids Camp, the river is wide and for the most part featureless, making it difficult for a newcomer to read. If the smolt are moving through, however, the birds and slashing trout obviate the need to read the water. Between schools of smolt, the best fishing is done with a heavy sinking-tip line and a leech, and a knowledge of the holding water is invaluable.

When the sockeyes move in, about June 20, the trout fishing begins to slack off. Whether because of pressure from the huge schools of salmon or the lack of food, the trout move back into the lake, and by mid-July, little if any trout fishing remains on the Naknek. But for anglers arriving in late June and early July, the sockeyes make up for it. The best fishing for sockeyes is from Rapids Camp upstream about four miles to a spot known as Preacher's Rock. Above that point, water conditions make it difficult to cast without snagging fish, always a problem with sockeyes.

Although the Naknek is a world-class king salmon river, little fly fishing is to be had. Anglers can target these fish in the few miles just above Rapids Camp, however, and kings are available in catchable numbers by the third week of June. There is a good catch-and-release king fishery on the Naknek's main tributary, Big Creek, which enters the river just below Rapids Camp.

Both kings and sockeyes spawn late in the Naknek, with the kings starting about the middle of August. The spawning salmon bring the trout back down out of the lake and the Naknek. The silvers show up at about the same time, and good fishing for cohos can be had from the third week in August until about September 10.

But it is the trout—more specifically, the big trout—that most fly fishers are after on the Naknek. The numbers of thirty-plus-inch fish increase as the season progresses. The trout are focused almost exclusively on eggs, both king and sockeye, until the kings begin to die in mid-September. This adds a new food source to the trout's diet, which helps break their sometimes very selective focus on eggs. Flesh patterns and leeches are alternatives to fishing Glo-Bugs or beads and can be more effective in covering broad stretches of water.

By October, the weather in Bristol Bay is cold and wet, reminiscent of winter steelhead conditions. The trout will also remind you of steelhead. Few anglers are seen on the river at this time of year, but those who make the journey are often rewarded with the fish of a lifetime. Most of the trout that spawn in the Naknek in May spend the winter in the river, hunkering down in the deep holes during freeze-up.

KVICHAK RIVER

The Kvichak rivals the Naknek as a big-fish destination. The fish here have all of the length of those in the Naknek, but many people claim that they have a broad-shouldered build that makes them even tougher than their cousins a few miles to the south.

Iliamna is by far the largest of the lakes in Bristol Bay, extending some eighty miles from the Chigmit Mountains to its outlet. Some of the best trout streams in the country, including the Copper, Lower Talarik Creek, and Gibraltar, flow into it. And the Kvichak flows out of it, crystal clear and a hundred yards wide. The tiny village of Igiugig sits at the mouth of the lake, and some massive rainbows can be caught alongside the boats and gear that line the riverbank. The Kvichak is about fifty miles long, but the fishing is concentrated in the upper twelve miles of river, from the lake down through a section called the braids. Some very productive fishing is found right at the lake's outlet, where a negligible current will slowly swing a pulsating leech or streamer past cruising trout.

Only a few large islands break the first five miles of river. The edges of these islands offer some shallow flats, and the rainbows move up onto them to chase sculpins, feed behind spawning salmon, or gorge on flesh, depending on the time of year. In most cases, there is good water at both the upper and lower ends of the islands.

The braids begin at Peck's Creek, one of the two major tributaries that flow into the upper river. The river passes around a maze of islands and widens dramatically, extending a full mile and a half from bank to bank. The many channels provide the best fishing in the river. Look for trout in the shallows, along the steep banks, and in the seams alongside the main current. Two other streams, Ole and Kaskanak Creeks, flow into the main river here. Good fishing can be had at the mouths of both of these streams. Below the braids, the river becomes deep, wide, and featureless. Although there are some large trout in this water, it is very difficult to fish with a fly.

Historically, the primary salmon species in the Kvichak has been sockeye. The escapement goal for the Iliamna drainage is two million fish, which is a substantial run. Unfortunately, the returns have fallen far short of that goal for the last few years.

A run of silvers arrives in mid-August and can often be found around the mouths of Kaskanak and Ole Creeks. Having said that, though, the Kvichak is not really a coho destination. The river also gets a large run of chums, which have provided food—and fishing—for trout with the crash of the sockeye stocks.

The Kvichak has a big smolt run in the early summer, but in warm years it often is over before the season opens. If the smolt have already moved out of the lake, some very good fishing still can be had by dredging the bottom with big leeches and sculpin patterns. Warm weather brings some surface activity, particularly with large attractor patterns. The river has some nice grayling that keep the surface action going, and every once in a while a rainbow will smack your dry fly.

Trout fishing slacks off during midsummer, as many of the fish move back up into the lake. Once the salmon start to spawn, the larger fish drop back down into the river, and by about the third week in August, the possibility of a thirty-incher begins to grow. Unlike the Naknek, the Kvichak has clear water, and under the right lighting conditions, it is possible to spot these fish. Egg patterns, usually beads, are a necessity for this period of time, but once the salmon start to die, flesh flies and leeches account for some big fish. As fall deepens, more and more of the big fish drop down into the main river. Late September is trophy time, and you'd better have a reel with a good drag. The Kvichak sees even fewer October anglers than the Naknek, but the fish are there.

ALAGNAK RIVER

The Alagnak is a bit different from the other two rivers of this triumvirate. There are no towns or villages nearby, and the fishable part of the river is much longer than the Kvichak or Naknek. The rainbows are not quite as big, but the salmon runs make up for any deficiencies.

The Alagnak drains two large lakes. The main stem, often called the Branch River, flows out of Kukaklek Lake. About five miles from the outlet of the lake, the river passes through a steep-walled canyon, and some significant rapids make the river a serious challenge for anyone who is not an experienced rafter. A lot of king salmon spawn in the upper stretches of the river, and they attract the big rainbows that drop out of the lake. About seventeen miles below the lake, the Branch meets the Nonvianuk River, which flows from a lake of the same name.

Nonvianuk Lake, like the other lakes, supports large numbers of salmon smolt, which make it prime rainbow habitat. The Nonvianuk River is much shorter than the Branch and lacks the whitewater challenge. As a result, most parties—guided and unguided—start their floats at Nonvianuk Lake. The Alagnak is perhaps the best entry-level river for someone looking for a Bristol Bay float. There are no gravel bars, so campsites are at a premium, but it has plenty of fish, few bears, and enough traffic on the river to provide a security blanket in the case of an emergency.

The best fishing on the Alagnak is a length of islands and channels that, like a similar stretch on the Kvichak, is known as the braids. Unlike the Kvichak's islands, these are generally brushy, and it's not always easy to find a spot from which to make a cast. Early-summer smolt fishing can be good, but don't restrict those patterns to just the first few weeks of the season. The smolt continue to outmigrate in the Alagnak system through mid-July. You'll also find good dry-fly action once the weather warms up, particularly with big attractors. Mice can be excitingly effective here as well.

The Alagnak gets a big run of sockeyes, and they can be targeted along the shallow bars and island edges. Sockeyes run along the edges of the rivers rather than in the main channel like kings. Find a corner at the right time and an unending stream of salmon will pass by, nose to tail, for as long as you are there.

This is one of the few rivers in the state where you can get a good shot at a king salmon on a fly rod. The bottom twelve-mile stretch of the river is shallow enough to work a fly down to the kings' depth, although most of the fishing is done by casting from an anchored boat. The kings begin to move into the river in early June, but the fishing peaks during the last half of July, later than on most rivers.

The Alagnak also has a big run of chums, a fish overlooked in most of its range. The lower river gets bright chrome fish and has two runs, in early July and early August. The best fishing for them is along the edges of slack water; they like the little sloughs and backwaters along the main river. Chums will hit a skated dry fly in much the same manner as silvers.

The silver run begins in early August and continues for about a month. They like flies that have some action to them and are stripped aggressively. The Alagnak was an early testing ground for fishing Pink Pollywogs, called Wogs for short, topwater skaters that have revolutionized fly-fishing for cohos. Few salmon experiences are more fun than watching a big buck coho follow a skated Wog through two or three casts before he engulfs it.

As on all of these rivers, the trout fishing peaks during and just after spawning season. The salmon spawn a bit later on the Alagnak, but the big run of kings means that there are eggs in the water before the sockeyes start. The Alagnak's clear water and braided channels make for excellent sight fishing. The key is not to look for the trout and Dollies, which are well camouflaged, but to cast behind the very obvious spawning salmon. If the river is clogged with spawners, concentrate on those areas where the current will wash the loose eggs down to good holding water. Chutes, drop-offs, and heavier water can be very good under these conditions.

The big rivers of Bristol Bay are not for everyone. They are hard to read, and casts need to be long to reach many of the best holding areas. But if you're looking for a trophy rainbow, there's no better place in North America to find one.

4

FISHING THE BIG RIVERS OF BRISTOL BAY
with Nanci Morris Lyon

With her trademark pink vest, Nanci Morris Lyon is perhaps the best known, and certainly one of the most respected, guides in Bristol Bay. Being female and attractive doesn't hurt, but Nanci earned her reputation by putting her clients on lots of very big fish. I have fished with Nanci on several occasions over the years, both on her home water, the Naknek, and on smaller streams. She knows her way around all of them, but it is her ability to find big trout on big rivers that stands out.

Nancy has been guiding in this area for eighteen years and has operated her outfitting business, Katmai Adventures, since the early nineties. She has a bit of advantage in finding big rainbows because she lives on the banks of the Naknek, and she knows it very well. That knowledge shows. Her largest rainbow was a thirty-seven-inch-long, twenty-two-and-a-half-pound monster taken a few years ago. Eight of her clients have landed thirty-six-inch fish, all from the Naknek.

Nanci lives in King Salmon with her husband, Heath, who has been guiding almost as long as she has. Her daughter, Rylie, age seven, is following in her mother's footsteps, with a fifty-five-pound king salmon and a thirty-two-inch rainbow already to her credit.

During the peak of the season, Nanci employs five or six other guides, fishing the Naknek with eighteen- and twenty-foot Willie Predators. For clients who want to venture farther afield, she will charter with Branch River Air to fish anyplace between Mother Goose Lake and the town of Nondalton.

Although some late-winter fishing can be had on the Naknek, Nanci's season begins in earnest in June. Opening Day for trout is June 8, and the fish are hungry. These early-season fish are postspawn and still a bit snaky. There is less food in the water than later in the season, and the fish are more opportunistic. But when the water warms and the smolt begin to move, hold on. I fished the Naknek on Opening Day with Nanci a few years ago and saw firsthand the excitement created when millions of young salmon begin migrating out to the ocean. Waves of year-old sockeyes, swimming high in the water column, moved downstream. As the schools swept past us, we threw smolt imitations into the swirling mass of salmon fleeing from the ravenous trout and screaming birds. It was a far cry from spring-creek rainbows sipping mayflies.

The smolt run is an early-season draw, but the timing varies from river to river. It begins in May on the Naknek and continues through July. On the Kvichak, it is much earlier and often is over before the season opens. The Alagnak has a long smolt run, with more topwater fishing available than on either of the other two rivers.

The sight of a rainbow feeding frenzy means that you can fish on top. Nanci likes to fish small Muddlers and even poppers. Most anglers fish unweighted streamers on floating lines. Fishing on the surface usually means more rainbows, although they run somewhat smaller than the fish taken on weighted flies.

Although the topwater action is great, early-season fishing more typically involves dredging the bottom, particularly on the Kvichak. Black and olive sculpin patterns, leeches, and Double Bunnies work well. Big fish mean big flies, and Nanci particularly likes String Leeches and Articulated Leeches that often exceed three inches in length. A 15-foot sinking-tip will get the fly down, and density-compensated lines seem to help get the proper drift. In the cold water of early June, resting fish are less likely to pursue a meal, and you need to work the water methodically. The fly should swim about six inches above the bottom.

"These fish aren't real aggressive in this cold water," Nanci says, "and they usually won't chase a fast-stripped fly. You want to twitch the fly just enough to give it some life."

By late June, the sockeyes begin to move into the rivers in force, headed for the spawning grounds. Although the vast majority of these fish move on through to the lakes and tributary streams, the big rivers get their share of spawners. Male sockeyes can be very aggressive when they are fighting for a mate, and the rainbows are no match for them. The Naknek trout simply move back up into the lake from about July 20 to August 5. On the Alagnak, look for trout in the back channels, riffles, or water that is too heavy to hold salmon. The Kvichak holds rainbows throughout the summer, but most of the larger fish move back up into the lake once the smolt are done.

It is the salmon that draw the fish from the lakes back down into the rivers. On the Naknek, the rainbows return to feed once the kings start to spawn. Kings prefer deeper, faster water than the sockeyes and are able to build their redds in heavier gravel.

"Most of our fishing in August is done in the heavier water behind the kings. But you want to methodically work your way out to the deeper water," Nanci says. "A lot of times these trout will move up into the shallows where they can find resting lies and get away from the salmon."

The Kvichak has no significant run of kings, so the larger trout tend to drop back into the river a little later in August, holding behind the spawning chums. Chums spawn in shallower, slower water than either kings or sockeyes. The trout are more vulnerable behind the chums and often hide under available cover, next to cut banks, or in the riffles below the spawning salmon. Just because you don't see trout behind the chums doesn't mean that they aren't around.

The sockeyes begin to spawn in late August, and the trout spread out onto the shallower spawning beds. The bigger fish, thirty-plus inches, also start to return to the river. The big fish begin to drop down out of the lakes about the last week in August, and Nanci says her clients on the Naknek usually hook one or two fish a week that push thirty inches. By the second week of September, the number of big fish hooked has increased to two or three a week, and by the last week of September and through the end of the season, someone hooks a trophy almost every day. A similar success ratio holds on the Kvichak. Fishing also peaks in the fall on the Alagnak, although the trout are not quite as large.

These big fish are in the river for one reason: to fatten themselves for winter on the glut of salmon eggs suddenly available. Like most trout guides in Alaska, Nanci fishes beads as egg patterns. Beads come in a number of colors, ranging from the hot orange of a fresh king egg through the dull, faded yellow of an infertile sockeye egg. As do many guides, Nanci coats them with a thin layer of pearlescent fingernail polish. Size is critical, with six- or eight-millimeter beads appropriate for sockeye eggs and the larger, ten-millimeter beads for fishing behind kings. With the right size and color combination, they are indistinguishable from the naturals. Nanci uses a nipped-off toothpick to peg them no more than two inches above a size 6 short-shank hook. Barbs are pinched down to facilitate releasing the fish.

In the clear waters of the Kvichak and Alagnak, trout can be very sensitive to color. Most guides carry boxes with as many as two dozen variations in order to match the prevailing color. Sometimes, though, it is better to give the fish something a bit different. The Alagnak and Kvichak get large runs of chum salmon, and the trout follow them into the shallows and backwaters in which they spawn. Nevertheless, Nanci thinks that rainbows prefer sockeye and king eggs to those of pinks or chums. Rather than attempt to match the hatch, as it were, she uses a sockeye or king egg imitation, saying that the trout will pick it out from among the naturals.

For those fly fishers who object to using beads, as well as those in south-central Alaska, where beads are illegal in fly-fishing-only waters, the traditional Glo-Bugs and Iliamna Pinkies will catch fish. Although the trout don't reject real flies as quickly as they do a hard bead, you still need the ability to detect an often subtle strike in order to be successful. Whether fishing beads or traditional flies, a floating line and strike indicator are essential. Either corkies or yarn will work as an indicator. Be careful with bright red corkies, particularly in shallow water. They don't necessarily spook the fish, but they definitely can draw the trout's attention away from the fly. Yarn is more sensitive to soft takes, but the amount needed to stay afloat with a heavy split shot sometimes proves impossible to cast. It's even worse on a windy day. Experienced anglers usually carry both.

As the season progresses, the type of fishing changes. In early September, Nanci does 90 percent of her fishing with eggs. By mid-September, though, the kings have started to die off, and flesh flies and Bunny Leeches come into their own. Nanci prefers big flies, like Articulated Leeches, with mix-and-match colors, such as dirty white and a bit of pink or peach. Many are tied with a weighted head, which not only gets the fly deep, but also helps give it that little bit of action that she likes. At times, she also adds a bead to the fly as an additional attractor. Flesh flies are not the only option in late season. Sculpins and big leeches in black and olive are also effective. That Alaskan icon, the purple Egg-Sucking Leech, also catches fish.

On these big rivers, with a lot of water to cover, Nanci likes to fish flesh flies on the swing. They should not be stripped, but just given a little twitch to make the bunny fur or marabou flutter in the current. Mending the line usually provides enough action. You should fish flesh flies deep—right on the bottom—with a sinking-tip line, and cover the water methodically, starting near shore.

The weather in October can be brutal. It's an opportunity to get a little more mileage out of those old neoprene waders, although lots of fleece and Gore-Tex will work fine. Fingerless gloves, warm caps, and serious raingear are de rigueur. Those disposable hand-warmer packets are very welcome. Try slipping one between your socks before you pull on your boots in the morning. Even in midsummer, these waters are cold, and good-quality waders and pile pants are essential.

You need some serious artillery on these rivers. On the Naknek, where big flies, lots of wind, and long casts are the norm, the best rod is probably an 8-weight or a Spey. Given the size of the fish and the power of the river, Nanci doesn't like her clients to go lighter than a 7-weight, unless they are skilled casters and, more important, adept at landing big fish quickly. Bring along a bigger rod for kings. Floating lines, miniheads, and a heavy sinking-tip are all useful, and you should be prepared to fish all of them as conditions change. One thing that you can leave at home is your net. Only the largest will hold fish of the size found here.

Because there are no bear problems on the Naknek or Kvichak, 12- to 15-pound-test tippet is best, allowing you to get the fish in fast without wearing them out and injuring them. (On rivers with large numbers of grizzlies, like Brooks and Moraine, it is often necessary to break off a trout to avoid having a bear steal it.) Nanci insists on clear tippet; brown Maxima would stand out in the clear waters of the Kvichak and Alagnak and in the slightly aquamarine Naknek. Nanci feels that fluorocarbon tends to fray on the rocks and isn't as reliable as monofilament. Fluorocarbon is almost impossible for the trout to see, however, and can be a necessity on a particularly tough fish. Tapered leaders are a waste of money when you are fishing the types of flies used here.

Finding fish in big rivers like the Naknek can be intimidating. Nanci's secret is to break the run down into smaller sections that are manageable and fish the water very methodically—cast, step, cast, step. Big trout are lazy—well, energy efficient. They like the soft water that comes from indentations and large rocks. The drop-offs from shoals provide some of the best holding water. Although the fish move around a lot, some holes and structure consistently hold fish, and the better the lie, the bigger the fish that will have claimed it. Seeing the river at very low water, as Nanci gets to do, provides a major advantage in locating productive structure.

The braids on the Alagnak and Kvichak provide structure that is easier to read than the flow of the Naknek, but the principles are the same. Look for trout at the heads and tailouts of the islands, particularly if there are spawning salmon; chums love these spots. Outside bends, where the water cuts a deeper channel along the bank, are good; just make sure that you adjust your weight or drift to compensate for the deeper, faster water. Midchannel shoals and rocks usually have a trout or two.

For a fly rodder, the big rivers of Bristol Bay are probably the best trophy trout fisheries in North America, particularly during the late season. But not everyone is looking for rainbows, and these rivers also produce some excellent salmon fishing. Although much of the salmon fishing is done with conventional gear, among the three rivers there are opportunities to take all five species of salmon on fly tackle.

Many visitors come to the state with only one goal in mind: to catch a king salmon. Both the Naknek and Alagnak have good runs of kings. The big water of the Naknek is not conducive to taking kings on a fly rod, but if you don't care about keeping the fish, you'll find some excellent catch-and-release king fishing up Big Creek, a tributary of the Naknek. The Alagnak, because it is smaller and braids up, offers much better fly fishing for kings. King salmon fishing begins about July 1 and runs through the month, with the season closing on July 31.

Like all king fishing, this is down and dirty. Heavy sinking-tips, up to 300 grain, are the order of the day, although it is possible to occa- sionally take kings on a floating line in parts of the Alagnak. Ten-weight rods are about right, and even they will get a workout if you hook a big chromer.

Kings can be very sensitive to color. Nanci likes pink, green, black, red, or combinations of them for the clear water of the Alagnak. Pink or cerise is the color of choice for tea-stained waters. Flies should be tied on 1/0 or 2/0 hooks. Flowing materials like marabou, bunny fur, or FisHair work best. Fish the flies on the swing, with just the occasional twitch to bring the material to life. Takes are very soft, so set the hook at the slightest hesitation.

The most abundant fish in these systems are sockeyes. They are in the Naknek in fishable numbers by about June 25, and fresh fish are available up until about July 20. The Alagnak fish arrive about a week later. The best fishing is in the Kukaklek and Nonvianuk branches of the Alagnak. The Kvichak, which historically has had very good runs of sockeyes, has seen a dramatic fall-off in numbers over the past decade.

Sockeyes are very reluctant to take a fly, but they make up for it by appearing in such huge numbers that the odds go way up. The vast majority of sockeyes that are caught have been lined—that is, the leader has drifted into the fish's mouth and the line has pulled tight, with the fly hooking the fish on the outside of the mouth. That's not to say that this is the only way sockeyes are caught. I've had a sockeye take a small streamer pattern fished in the surface film. Nevertheless, the key to catching these salmon is to get the fly and leader moving through the school at exactly the right depth. Weight and leader length are critical.

The best sockeye fishing is found in shallow water with a significant current. An inside bend where the fish are forced to cut across a shallowing bar is ideal. Although large bucktails are common in many areas, Nanci much prefers to use a large, size 6 beadhead nymph or comet-type fly. Color is of little importance. Sockeyes tend to run up the river fairly close to shore, so short casts are all that's required. Set the hook when the line stops.

The most underappreciated fish in Bristol Bay is undoubtedly the chum salmon. They are big, tough, and aggressive. The Alagnak is one of the best chum streams around, but they are also available in Big Creek and the Kvichak. Chums color up fast after hitting fresh water, but bright fish are available from about July 7 to August 7. The Alagnak actually has two runs of chums, the first arriving in early July and the second a month later.

An 8-weight rod and 20-pound-test leader is about right for these fish. Flies are similar to those used for kings, but chums can be sensitive to both size and color, so be prepared to change if they're not hitting. Nanci likes Bunny Flies tied in green or pink. Leeches and Zonker style flies work well, particularly with lots of marabou in the tail. Chums seem to like more flash in the fly than do kings. Although they sometimes will take a dead-drifted fly, Nanci likes to give it more action than she would for kings.

Chums will also take a skated surface fly. Bombers, poppers, Waller Wakers, and Pink Pollywogs are all good patterns. Look for a large group of fish holding in a gently moving pool, and fish the fly with sudden jerks, as erratically as possible. Again, color and size can be important, so change flies if it's not working.

Without question, silvers are the favorite salmon of most fly fishers. These are not destination rivers for cohos, but they are nevertheless available in all three. They arrive about August 10 in the Naknek and about a week later in the Kvichak and Alagnak. That same 8-weight rod you need for trout will work on silvers.

Although silvers like deep, slow pools, Nanci believes that the best fishing is often found in moving water. They tend to get lockjaw very quickly in stillwater. Silvers are very spooky, and anglers need to stay back from the fish. Walking along a high bank will cause every fish to move out into deep water.

Cohos are very color conscious, and changing flies until you find one that works is important. If the fish go off that color, try something new. Nanci likes purple, red, orange, pink, and chartreuse. She says that if you make three casts into a pod of fish without drawing a strike, it's time to change flies. Size can also be important, so carry some flies as small as size 6. Regardless of what you use, cohos are notorious for suddenly turning off and on. Sometimes you just need to go have lunch and come back after they've had a mood swing.

Silvers like a fly with action. Strip it and use lots of variation in the retrieve. They are much more likely to move sideways than up to take a fly, although they can be annoyed into hitting a skated dry fly. Rather than cast over a pod of fish, drop the fly alongside them. Usually you can get a fish to peel off and hit it. Silvers are aggressive and will usually hit a fly within the first couple casts. Don't stand in one spot and continue casting to the same fish; it's far more productive to keep moving between casts.

The most exciting way to take silvers is undoubtedly on the surface. Nanci says that the rules change for dry flies. "Sometimes it seems like you have to tease the fish into hitting. It may take fifteen to twenty casts to get a fish to come up to the fly. Try popping the fly to begin, and then start sliding it. Be erratic in your retrieve. Usually you will first see a wake behind the fly as a fish follows it. A boil on the fly, without the fish actually taking it, may come next. When the fish hits, though, you'll know it."

The most common mistake people make when fishing these rivers, she says, is that "too many people like to stand in one spot. You need to keep moving. It doesn't matter whether you're fishing for rainbows or salmon, use the cast-step technique and cover the water."

The Naknek, Kvichak, and Alagnak are probably the only three rivers in the country where, at the right time of year, you have a realistic chance at catching a native rainbow that exceeds ten pounds. The techniques and timing are critical, but if you're looking for that once-in-a-lifetime trophy, this is the place to come.

5

SOUTHWEST ALASKA

Beyond Katmai, west of the Nushagak and the beautiful Wood River system, lie the rivers of Kuskokwim Bay. The Kanektok, Aniak, and a handful of lesser-known streams provide an opportunity to spend a week or so floating from the alpine cirques of the high country to the lowlands of the coastal plain. This is Alaska unspoiled. The fishing for salmon, trout, and char is some of the finest in the state. Wolf and bear tracks mark the riverbank mud, and caribou range the ridgetops. Far from the fabled waters of the Bristol Bay, this area sees fewer anglers than any other rainbow habitat in the state. Facilities are more rustic, and even though transportation is by boat rather than floatplane, it is still possible to float almost a hundred miles on some streams and not see another angler.

Southwest Alaska marks the outer limits of the rainbow trout's range. Rivers here flow from the peaks of spectacular ranges like the Kilbucks and Ahkluns to sea level, either meeting the Bering Sea or dumping into the Kuskokwim, a massive riverine highway that provides a transportation system for the entire area. The fish are perhaps a bit smaller and not as numerous as their better-known cousins in Bristol Bay, but they are hard fighters and eager to eat a fly.

The days are long gone when these rivers were secret—when the Kanektok was referred to as the Chosen River, fabled but misidentified. Now it and its sister rivers, such as the Goodnews, Arolik, Aniak, and Kisaralik, are tucked away on the Alaska aficionado's dream list. But even if they are no longer unknown, they still require a sense of adventure to explore them properly. Unlike the small streams of Bristol Bay, where an angler can fly in during the day and be back at the lodge for a gourmet dinner in the evening, these are boating rivers. And although camps run river boats upstream from the lower stretches on some of them, the best way to see most of these gems is by floating their entire length.

These rivers do not have the large midsystem lakes common to the Bristol Bay streams and consequently do not support the large runs of sockeyes that dominate the food chain in that area. They do, however, get big runs of kings, chums, and silvers, which spawn pretty much throughout their length, and the salmon support healthy populations of trout and Dolly Varden.

This is probably the best area in the state to catch kings on a fly rod, particularly in the Kanektok and Aniak. Unlike the other major king salmon rivers, such as the Nushagak and Kenai, these streams are a manageable size. They have gravel bottoms and a moderate to swift flow, perfect water for a fly rod. As with all chinook fisheries, the key is to get the fly right on the bottom. Kings rarely move up to take a fly, and you usually need to bump them on the nose. These are small enough rivers that a sinking-tip line and weighted fly will allow you to do that. Kings begin entering the rivers in the latter part of June, with the best fishing coming in July.

Most of these streams have some very good chum runs, and although many Alaskan fishers treat these fish with disdain, they are incredibly tough if you get them when they're bright. Chums enter the rivers in early July but tend to color up fairly quickly.

The real prize comes in August, when the cohos begin to run. With the trout fishing at its peak, arriving anglers can keep their arms sore for a week. The Kanektok and Goodnews see their biggest crowds at this time of year, and good fishing can be had in the Aniak. This region is probably not the best in the state as a pure coho destination, but they certainly add to the excitement of exploring the area.

The rainbows in these rivers are among the most beautifully colored anywhere, with scarlet stripes and such heavy spotting that they are universally referred to as leopard bows. They are aggressive and far less sophisticated than the fish found in the Katmai and Iliamna drainages. As on all Alaskan trout water, eggs, flesh, and sculpins are the usual flies of choice, but this is also great mousing country. Few fishing experiences are more exciting than watching big rainbows attack a skated Deerhair Mouse. And *attack* is the operative word—no delicate dry-fly sipping here. These fish have no intention of letting a meaty intruder escape.

Rainbows are the prime target here, but most places have more Dollies than trout. These Dollies are not the snaky sixteen-inchers that are common in many areas. Most of these fish have the length, if not the girth, of the rainbows, and by August the males are so colored up that they put even the leopard bows to shame. They will hit any fly used for rainbows, but they are suckers for egg patterns.

By far the best way to enjoy these rivers is by floating them. All of them start high in the mountains, flowing out of their natal lakes as tiny, rock-strewn creeks. This is dry tundra, with nothing larger than the scrawny willows that line the creekbed, and the first few miles usually require dragging the boats through some of the shallows. The steep, rocky drainages quickly fill the streams, though, and they are easily floatable after the first day. The fishing is usually mediocre to poor at the upper elevations, with little more than a scattering of grayling. The Dollies start to appear with the first significant numbers of salmon, but the good trout action doesn't come until you begin to drop out of the foothills. Camping is almost always on gravel bars, and the fishing is usually just a cast in front of the tents. With a couple exceptions, these are technically easy rivers, but they are all serious wilderness, and a rafter needs the skill and experience to be completely self-reliant. You can't change your mind and go home two days into the trip.

Caribou roam the tundra-covered ridges of the high country, and it's not unusual to see bands moving through on a regular basis or round a corner and come upon a young bull standing splay-legged and surprised in the middle of the river. With the caribou come wolves. Their surprisingly large tracks trace the muddy outlines of the banks, and if you're lucky, you'll hear their calls serenade the evening.

As the rivers pass from the hills out onto the tundra and begin to flatten out, they start to braid up. Cottonwoods and willows line the banks, and sweepers and logjams begin to appear. This is prime rainbow country, and the side channels and back sloughs are always worth exploring. Spawning salmon, usually kings or chums, are the most obvious indicator of good trout fishing. Keep in mind that this is also prime bear country. Although the populations are not as large as those found farther east, these bears are not as habituated to people, and the brushy country will allow you to get way too close to a bear before either of you realizes it.

At the lower end, these rivers become slowly meandering streams, drifting between banks of mud. The fishing is essentially over at this stage, so you don't want to spend any more time than necessary on that last stretch of water. Depending on the river, a powerboat pickup can save you a day or more of hard rowing into the prevailing wind. Some of these rivers have permanent camps or lodges, usually situated upstream from the sloughlike conditions near the mouth.

Whether you float the entire river or powerboat up from the lower river for day trips, there is one constant to all of these streams: They are right in the path of the big low-pressure troughs that come sweeping off the Bering Sea. Plan for bad weather every day of the trip, and you will be adequately prepared—and pleasantly surprised by the sunshine between storms. This is not country where you can get away with cheap raingear or cotton clothing. Fleece and Gore-Tex will be your everyday wear on most trips. If you are camping on the gravel bars, make sure you have a tarp and a bullet-proof way to rig it as a shelter for cooking, eating, and waiting out the weather. I use the raft and rowing frame as the upwind anchor on the tarp. It might flap, but it won't blow away. Freestanding tents built to withstand mountain winds will let you sleep better at night.

There is a certain similarity to these rivers, but each has its own character. The ones described below are the best known, but others, such as those named at the end of the chapter, can provide fishing and camping that are every bit as good, with even fewer people.

KANEKTOK RIVER
The most popular float trip in southwest Alaska is on the Kanektok, and this river deserves its reputation. It is a crystal-clear, gravel-bottomed stream that, at least under normal water conditions, poses no serious technical challenges. Beginning at Kagati Lake in the Ahklun Mountains, it flows about ninety miles to its mouth at the village of Quinhagak. It has lots of gravel bars, and camping is easy. The upper portion of the river is in a wilderness-designated area, where motors are not

allowed. The best fishing, however, begins below the wilderness boundary. There are no places to land a plane or take out on the river, so a float trip is an all-or-nothing proposition.

The Kanektok has large populations of all species of salmon, good rainbows, lots of char, and hungry grayling. It may be the best river in the state for catching king salmon on a fly rod, with fish ranging from eighteen to thirty pounds. It also has a reputation as a great river for fishing a mouse for char and rainbows. The trout typically run from eighteen to twenty-two inches, with char about the same size. Fishing for rainbows begins to get good in late July, when the kings start making their redds.

The Kanektok has taken its rightful place as one of Alaska's premier destination rivers. Remote, scenic, and full of fish—it epitomizes what many people think of when they dream of an Alaskan trip.

ANIAK RIVER

The Aniak is something of an anomaly among the rivers of southwest Alaska. Unlike the other streams, which provide relatively easy floats and have shallow spawning beds and open tundra, the Aniak is a river not lightly undertaken. Whether you begin in the more popular Salmon River or the difficult upper Aniak, the upper stretches are full of sweepers, logjams, and bears. The lower half of the river, below the confluence of the Salmon, Aniak, and Kipchuk, is not any easier. A big, fast river, the Aniak braids up into twisting channels that weave through an ever-changing cottonwood forest. Deep water strewn with snags and sweepers makes the fishing a dream and the navigation a nightmare.

The Aniak provides big rewards for those who venture there, though. It gets a good run of kings, and fishing in late June and early July is very productive. Chums arrive a bit later than the kings, and although few people target them, they draw the rainbows up from the deep, heavy water of the main river into the sloughs and back channels that the salmon use for spawning. By early August, the silvers begin to show up, hanging in the numerous areas of slow water. Although the Aniak is at the extreme end of the rainbows' range, the trout are large, strong, and willing. These are the same heavily spotted leopard bows that occur in the other drainages of the Kuskokwim.

In spite of its difficulties, the Aniak is one of the more heavily fished rivers in the area, partly a function of direct jet service from

Anchorage to the village of Aniak. Several lodges operate in the area and run jet boats up into the lower stretches of the river. For the experienced wilderness paddler, the float trip is an adventure that few people will ever have the opportunity to partake in.

GOODNEWS RIVER

The Goodnews is one of the sweetest little streams in Alaska, with beautiful scenery in the upper ends and consistently good fishing, and it's less crowded than the Kanektok. Like the Kanektok, it's a river that's best floated, although outfitters maintain camps at the lower end. The Goodnews is actually two separate rivers—the main stem and the Middle Fork—which come together only a short distance above tidewater. Both are shallow, clear streams that originate in the Ahklun Mountains.

The upper stretches of both streams require a bit of work. The Middle Fork is shallow and rocky and requires a bit of dragging the first day out. The main stem has a long, slow stretch with little camping available for the first four miles. Once the rivers pick up additional water, they become fine rivers for floating. As with most of the rivers in this area, the upper miles are fast and scenic, but the fishing, at least for rainbows, is sporadic. Once you drop out of the foothills, though, the Goodnews comes into its own as a fishing destination. The deep channels hold good runs of silvers, and there are plenty of fat, darkly spotted rainbows and eager char. Most of the char are searun Dollies that show up about mid-July. The lower stretches have good fishing for kings, and the river is small enough that a fly rod is an adequate weapon for them.

OTHER RIVERS

This is not an exhaustive list of the rivers in southwest Alaska. The Kisaralik, Arolik, Kwethluk, Holitna, and others still provide opportunities for anglers to explore little-known watersheds and find good fishing.

For many Alaskan fly fishers, tired of the crowds of Bristol Bay and the south-central region, southwest Alaska is a favorite refuge. At its best, the trout and salmon fishing rivals any place in the state, and the scenery and wildlife, particularly in the high country, are spectacular. For those looking for the quintessential wilderness experience and good fishing to go along with it, few options are better than a float trip in Southwest Alaska.

6

FLOATING RIVERS
with Chuck Ash

Floating through eighty or a hundred miles of wilderness, sleeping on gravel bars, and taking whatever nature brings may not be for everyone, but it has an intensity that can't be matched by any fancy lodge. It has long been my favorite way to fish Alaskan rivers. Although floatable rivers exist throughout the state, without question the best are found in southwest Alaska. They are the right size for fly fishing; they are located in true wilderness areas, where the only buildings are a few native fish camps complete with drying racks lined with the winter's supply of salmon; and they have some of the best fishing available in Alaska. Only a limited number of guides specialize in these trips, and Chuck Ash is among the best.

Chuck has guided fly fishers in Alaska for more than thirty years. Sixty years old, he is still lean and whip-tough—a necessity for anyone who focuses on his type of guiding. A trip with him is a weeklong magical tour of an entire ecosystem, mountains to ocean. Chuck floats some of the most beautiful wilderness trout streams in the world, primarily the Goodnews and Mulchatna Rivers, although he has also offered trips on the Togiak and Alagnak. He is also one of the finest pure fly fishers in the business—good enough that he was inducted as a legendary guide into the Freshwater Fishing Hall of Fame.

Chuck lives in Anchorage and spends his winters on cross-country skis—that is, when he's not chasing bonefish or permit from the Bahamas to the Seychelles. He's a former schoolteacher with a degree in biology and a minor in conservation. In his teaching days, he offered a popular course called applied freshwater ecology—and yes, it included tying flies to match the various prey species. It's unlikely that you will find another guide in the state with an equivalent breadth of knowledge.

The rivers of southwest Alaska typically do not have the lake system of Bristol Bay, so they lack the massive runs of sockeyes found in those rivers. Kings, chums, and silvers predominate, and the trout fishing largely occurs on the spawning beds of these species. Without the lakes in which to overwinter, the trout drop down to the deep lower stretches of the rivers in the fall and remain there until the first waves of migrating kings draw them upriver.

The fishing on these rivers begins about July 1. The kings are entering the river, and the water levels have dropped to manageable proportions. Early in the season, the best fishing is found in the lower stretches of the rivers, giving an advantage to the fixed base camps located near the mouths of most of these streams. By the third week in July, though, the trout have moved upstream, the rivers are flush with salmon, and the fall-spawning Dollies have entered fresh water. From then until early September, a float trip will allow you to experience Alaska as you have always imagined it to be.

Float trips are unique, but that's not the only reason I asked Chuck to participate in this book. The techniques he uses are different from those of many other guides. They require a bit more skill, but in the hands of a good fly fisher, they are both more effective and more in keeping with traditional methods. Throughout Chuck's discussion of fishing for various species, he refers to fishing with a floating line, often in situations where most guides would insist on a deep-dredging sinking-tip line or a heavy weight and strike indicator. Chuck likes to use as little weight as possible and prefers the weight to be in the fly itself, rather than use split shot.

By using a floating line and long leader, he feels that he can get a better drift. There is less drag, and the fly stays in the fish's zone longer. The fly won't sink under the fish or hang up on the bottom. He also knows exactly where the fly is—just upstream from the line. And by keeping the line tight, he can detect strikes, both by feel and by the movement of the fly line, from even those fish that simply mouth the fly, like kings and sockeyes.

Chuck explains his technique: "You need to cast far enough above the productive part of the run to allow the fly to sink into the fish's zone. Mend the line whenever it's necessary. Unlike dry-fly fishing, you are looking for a dead drift without the S curves of tippet. It helps to draw the line in very slowly—just enough to keep in touch with the fly and know when it stops."

Chuck's methods were refined on the shallow, gravel-bottomed, clear-water streams of western Alaska, but they are equally effective on any of the smaller rivers that have similar characteristics. There is a bit of a learning curve, but the results are rewarding.

These rivers have the full range of species, and Chuck has specific and sometimes unique techniques for each of them. Let's start with trout and Dollies. As soon as you see the first one, you will understand how they came by the name leopard bows. Most of them run in the low- to mid-twenty-inch range—a bit smaller than their cousins in Bristol Bay, but still very respectable fish. They begin to move up the river with the first salmon, and by the third week in July, they are well distributed throughout the drainage.

These early-season fish gather around the spawning beds, but they are not yet keyed on eggs. Woolhead Sculpins, Egg-Sucking Leeches, and Woolly Buggers are all effective. Chuck likes a black or olive bead leech, tied with a mohair body, a Zonker strip, and a black tungsten bead. Small baitfish patterns are also useful for imitating the outgoing smolt. In odd years, when a large number of pink salmon eggs are hatching, a size 6 white smolt pattern can be very effective. Dry flies are also good during the midsummer period. Caddis patterns are the match-the-hatch choice, but Chuck's favorite is a Royal Wulff.

The most famous pattern for these fish is the Deerhair Mouse. These rivers are the best in the state for mousing, and no angler should go there without a box of these flies. The proper pattern is critical for success, but that does not mean those cute, little deer-hair imitations that look like they would steal cheese. The commercial ties usually have a pointy nose—very lifelike, but it causes the fly to dive rather than skate. A blunt-nosed or foam-backed pattern fishes much better, and a thin profile is easier to cast and fish. Chuck likes to tie his on up-eye salmon hooks to keep the head up. I have used riffle hitches, with the hitch tied under the throat of the fly, for the same reason. Trout tend to viciously inhale an escaping mouse, and stinger hooks will help keep the fish from taking the fly too deep.

There are two ways to fish mice. The first is to hit the bank and strip slowly, swimming the fly away from the grass. In faster water, move the fly just fast enough that it will escape if the fish hesitates; don't give it time to think about it. A regular quartering downstream cast and swing are usually effective, although you may have to adjust the speed of the swing. Fish will often hit just as the fly stops at the end of the swing, the same reaction you expect when fishing streamers. One of Chuck's favorite techniques is to swim the mouse alongside a rock and then move it out of the current into the eddy behind the rock.

Once the salmon begin to spawn, the mousing and streamer fishing are essentially over. The fish are looking for their primary food of the summer and are keyed on eggs. Many of Chuck's techniques and strategies are unique, but his biggest departure from his fellow guides is his opposition to fishing beads. Beads are very controversial among Alaskan fly fishers. They allow unskilled anglers to catch a lot of big rainbows, and the guides typically use them because of the economic competition among lodges.

Beads are effective for two reasons. First, a properly colored bead is almost indistinguishable from a real egg. You can't tell them apart in your hand, and a fish certainly can't differentiate between the real thing and the fake—until, of course, it has it in its mouth. Egg-eating rainbows spend a lot of time picking up eggs from the gravel, and they become very sensitive to anything hard, rejecting it immediately. Beads attached to the hook are not very effective for that reason. It is almost impossible to detect the strike before the fish has spit out the fly—and a bead attached to a hook meets the definition of fly, at least as set out in the Alaskan regs.

But beads are not attached to the hook. They are fixed on the leader with a toothpick peg, by regulation no more than two inches above the fly. Pegging is deadly because it effectively prevents the fish from rejecting the bead. As the fish spits out the bead, the tippet drags through its mouth, hooking it almost automatically—or as critics put it, snagging the fish. If you put a big strike indicator on the line, the drag on the indicator will even set the hook automatically for you, eliminating the need for any skill beyond getting a good drift. It's not surprising that the guides, whose clients want to catch a lot of fish, feel the need to use beads.

Chuck Ash is one of the very few that don't. "I just think that fly fishing should be done with a real fly. But my primary concern is that the injury rate with beads is higher. A pegged bead will swing the hook around and snag the fish in the face, often in the eye. The resource has to come first. It's a blood sport, so you have to minimize the impact."

The implementation of the two-inch rule was designed to minimize injuries, but it hasn't eliminated them. Most of the trout are hooked on the outside of the mouth, in the mandible. On rivers that are heavily fished with beads, it's rare to find a fish that isn't missing at least one mandible.

Using a real fly doesn't mean that Chuck's clients are missing out on the fish. He likes an egg pattern that he calls Billy's Krystal Egg. It is essentially a Glo-Bug tied with Iliamna pink McFly foam, a tungsten bead, and a few strands of pink pearlescent Krystal Flash as a tail. Occasionally he will fish a shade paler or, more rarely, a bit darker. The client who first showed him this fly took seventy fish on it the first day. The tungsten bead is the key, allowing the fly to get down to the bottom without the need of extra weight, which screws up the drift and interferes with detecting the strike.

For most southwest Alaskan fishing, Chuck prefers a 5-weight rod, although a 6-weight can come in handy if the wind is blowing or you are using bulky flies. For those systems with a lake, and consequently larger trout, a 6- or 7-weight works best. Chuck likes to use a floating line with a 9- to 12-foot leader, fished without an indicator whenever possible. He feels that he can get a better drift and keep the fly in the zone longer with a tight-line dead drift. With no additional weight and no indicator, these are techniques designed for skinny water.

Chuck's techniques are deadly in the right hands, but they do require a level of skill that new anglers haven't yet mastered. For those who have difficulty getting the fly deep enough or are missing too many strikes, he will add weight or an indicator as required. And if the client is really having a difficult time, he does have a few beads and toothpicks as a fallback.

Once the salmon have started to die, flesh flies become more important. Unlike the very large patterns that fill the boxes in the fly shops, Chuck likes a size 6 and sometimes a size 8 fly tied with white or ginger bunny fur as the body and a strip of shell pink fur as the tail.

He carries both heavily and lightly weighted patterns, distinguished by thread color, for varying conditions. Another pattern that is useful for special occasions is a Maggot Fly, simply a curved size 14 scud hook wrapped with white latex or dental floss. When a heavy rain raises the otherwise low water and washes carcasses into the river, the trout are used to seeing clouds of the white worms drifting along the edges and downstream from the bars. This is a particularly good fly for sight-fishing a difficult trout.

Once the spawning is over and the carcasses have started to disappear, the trout drop downstream quickly. By September, the rainbows are gone from the spawning beds. There is still fishing in the lower stretches of the rivers, where the fish are gorging on dead salmon in preparation for another winter under the ice.

Mixed in with the rainbows on all of these rivers are large numbers of Dolly Varden. Most people simply use the same techniques for Dollies as they do for trout, but Chuck points out some subtle differences that can be important. The most obvious is timing. Because the southwest Alaskan Dollies are almost wholly anadromous, they are not present in the river during the early part of the season. They start to arrive about the third week in July. They also are fall spawners and consequently remain in the upper river flats well after the rainbows have dropped out.

Late-season Dollies will still take egg patterns, but there are better flies. A size 6 Egg- Sucking Leech is the standard. Dollies are suckers for brighter flies, and Chuck likes a Mickey Finn, often tied with a beadhead. Royal Coachman streamers or pink and white Woolly Buggers are also good. Cast these flies cross-stream and allow them to dead drift until the line tightens and the fly swings across the current. Let the fly come to a stop, and then strip about a foot and let it hang. Keep repeating that strip-and-hang technique through the good water. Dollies can also be a great dry-fly fish when the mood strikes them. There are often some decent *Baetis* hatches on the char flats in late summer, so carry a few size 14 or 16 Adams in case you get lucky.

Grayling are common in all of these streams. No one actually travels to areas this remote looking for them, but they become the target species on some days, at least on float trips. The very upper stretches of these rivers provide spectacular scenery and wildlife viewing but few trout or char. Grayling will give you an opportunity to get the fly rods out on that first evening in camp. Carry a few size 14 and 16 caddis patterns in tan and green and some size 16 and 18 in black. A black A. P. Nymph fished as a dropper will pick up fish. Don't forget a spool of tippet material small enough to go through the eyes of these flies.

Trout are a big draw, but these rivers provide wonderful opportunities to take all species of salmon on a fly. Cohos are the most important here. They come into the rivers at the same time the trout fishing peaks, giving anglers a double bonus. The fish begin to move into the lower river during the last week in July. The best fishing in the upper rivers runs from the second week in August through the first week in September.

As with the rest of his fishing, Chuck prefers a floating line for silvers, although sinking-tips are sometimes necessary to get the fly deep enough. Unlike most salmon, he says, silvers will move up through the water column to take a fly, so getting the fly on the bottom is not as critical as it is with kings or sockeyes. It also means that you can take cohos on the surface under the right conditions.

Look for silvers in the frog water—those slow back eddies out of the main current. The fish will bunch up in these areas and tend to be more aggressive. The best fishing for silvers, even more than for most species, is early and late. They are very sensitive to bright sun, and the lower the light, the better.

The flies Chuck uses for silvers are almost always bright colors, and he says that a two-tone contrasting fly is better than a single color. The fly has to have movement, from either bunny fur or marabou, and it should have some flash. The all-flash flies, although popular in many areas, are less effective than a mixture of materials. Egg-Sucking Leeches—in black and lime, purple and pink, and white with either fuchsia or lime—are very good. Chuck also likes a saltwater pattern called Tabory's Snake. It's not durable, but it's unweighted and has lots of movement. Silvers can be very fickle, so if you're not getting action after half a dozen casts over a pod of fish, change flies.

In the slow water that silvers prefer, Chuck starts with a strip-and-pause retrieve. Try a medium to slow strip of about a foot and a one- or two-second pause. Silvers require a lot more action on the fly than any of the other salmon (sockeyes want the least). The first cast has the best chance of getting a hit. Chuck says that silvers like erratic action, and you can move quickly through the school looking for a player.

"If what you're doing doesn't work in short order, or if a fish moves to the fly but doesn't strike, change the tempo. You can change the speed of the strip, the length of the strip, or the amount of pause time. When the fly moves, it will often elicit a chase, but the takes usually come on the pause, and the fish will let go before the next strip. If you are not feeling the strikes, change to a short beat on the pause to prevent the fish from spitting out the fly before you can set the hook."

If you find silvers jammed into a fairly slow current, try using a surface fly. Much like mousing trout, silvers will come up to a skated dry. Pink Pollywogs and pink mouse patterns both work. Carrying both types gives you the option of a pattern that creates a lot of turbulence, such as a hammerhead Wog, or a fly that has a bullet head and thus causes a more subtle disturbance. When tying either of these flies, Chuck says to pack the deer hair as tightly as possible, and soak the fly in floatant. He likes to tie them on stinger hooks; they have a bigger gape, and the lighter wire won't sink the hook.

Silvers may be the money fish, but these rivers provide perhaps the best fly fishing for king salmon in the state. These are small-water kings and perfect for a fly rod. Most run between 15 and 30 pounds and can be handled on a 9- or 10-weight rod. More important, they are found in water that can be readily fished with a fly. Fishing for kings begins about July 1 in these rivers and continues until the end of the month. The opportunity is there, but don't get the idea that it's easy, even with a guide as experienced as Chuck Ash. "Sockeyes and kings are the two toughest fish to fish for in Alaska," he says. "It takes good technique to get the fly in the zone and good touch to feel the take. Kings just mouth the fly, so it takes a real touch to feel them."

Chuck's technique for kings is different from that used by guides on larger rivers and frankly a lot more fun. He likes to use a floating line with a leader up to 15 feet long. A minitip or regular sinking-tip is used to get the fly deeper in the larger holes. He fishes a dead drift with a tight line, occasionally giving it a long strip and then holding it. This technique requires a fly with a lot of inherent motion—the type of action that comes from bunny fur, arctic fox, or marabou. Using only minimal weight requires more skill in order to get the fly down into the fish's zone, but it allows you to sense the take. Less experienced anglers will require more weight or a heavier tip. If you aren't getting strikes and you can't feel the fly ticking the bottom, add a bit more lead.

The best fishing for kings is early or late in the day and on overcast days. "The fish just seem to go deep and off the bite on bright days," Chuck says. He fishes kings only in the holes, where they can hold in schools. The more thickly stacked up the fish are, the better. One of the advantages of rivers like the Goodnews and Kanektok is that they give you a chance to sight-fish for them. You can watch the fish's reaction to the pattern and techniques, changing them as necessary.

Probably the most-used fly for kings is a Fat Freddie. Chuck ties them in size 1 (a bit smaller than most) and fishes them dead drift. He also likes Egg-Sucking Leeches, particularly with a big, puffy head. Purple and pink are not the only useful color combination; black with a hot lime nose and white and lime are equally effective. Bunny Flies tied in size 2, in lime, black, or fuchsia, are also good, and you can add an enameled bead on the nose to weight it. A hot pink Woolly Bugger with bead-chain eyes is another deadly pattern. Chuck has one other fly that he keeps in his box: a size 4 black Sparkle Nymph. "It's not often, but when it's the right fly, it's the right fly."

One of the delights of an early-season float trip is sockeye fillets cooked over the coals. These rivers don't get the type of sockeye runs found in Bristol Bay, but there are still plenty of fish in most of the streams. They arrive with the kings and chums, showing up in the lower rivers by July 1. Sockeyes tend to migrate close to the banks and come in pulses, with fish showing up in bunches. Look for fish holding in the current breaks, behind a rock or gravel bar. Finding the fish bunched up is important.

Like most good sockeye fishers, Chuck likes small flies, size 6 or 8. Flies with a little weight are best. He likes Brassies (salmon Brassies, not the midge imitations) in white, pink, and lime; Gold Comets; and bonefish flies, such as Crazy Charlies. Sockeye oranges and greens are productive. He's also had good luck with a small nymph tied with a red floss body and peacock herl head.

Chuck uses a 7- or 8-weight rod and prefers a floating line when he can find the fish bunched up in shallow water. Fluorocarbon leaders are tough and sink faster than nylon and should be adjusted for the speed and depth of the water. Nine feet is a good starting length. The most effective technique is a tight-line dead drift, using the line as an indicator. It's critical to keep the fly just above the bottom, so don't keep the line so tight that it raises the fly up into the water column.

The most common mistake anglers make when targeting sockeyes is failing to get the fly deep enough. The second problem is wading out into the stream. These fish are holding in close to the shore and are spooky, particularly around large, land-based mammals. Wading out into the best water will make them go close-mouthed.

Chum salmon are a staple in most of these rivers. "Chums are easy," Chuck says. "They will hit anything with movement and color." He uses Egg-Sucking Leeches, lime or fuchsia Bunny Flies, or anything that is pink and sparkly. Size 4 hooks are about right. An 8-weight rod with a floating line and a long leader will get the fly into the zone, and he fishes with either a dead drift or a strip-and-pause technique. Like other species of salmon, chums are more susceptible when they are jammed up. Their aggression level goes up. They are also very aggressive when they get on the spawning beds, which can be a problem if you are targeting trout and tie into a slug-it-out chum.

FLOAT TRIPS

Float trips include far more than just fishing. These are true wilderness expeditions—no floatplanes landing next to you, no casting to fish that have been watching flies drift by them for weeks. Of course, they also mean no hot showers at the end of the day and no soft bed to crawl into when it's raining. Float trips are great, far more rewarding than any other method of fishing Alaska. But to enjoy them to the fullest requires a good attitude and, unless you're experienced in wilderness travel, a good guide. The attitude is up to you, but there are some things to look for in selecting a guide.

Chuck says that the first step is finding someone who enjoys being a float-trip guide. Too many operators use float trips as a second option for their clients, and they use their least experienced guides, who often view them as only a way to work up to the fly-out trips and hot showers. A guide who is passionate about this type of trip and does them exclusively will almost always provide a better experience. Not only will he have better interpretive skills, spotting wolf tracks or a gyrfalcon nest, but he will also be more attuned to the seasonal changes in the river. Fish, both salmon and trout, migrate dramatically, and the best areas for fishing change over the course of the season. Spend too much time above the fish and you have fewer opportunities when the fishing suddenly improves. Go past the best fishing and you're cooked.

A good float guide will be happy to explain everything about the trip before you put your money down. You should know what's being provided and what you're expected to bring. Like all reputable outfitters, Chuck provides top-quality rafts and gear. Equipment failure can leave you wet and cold. A large tarp for the kitchen provides a place out of the rain, and separate tarps for the tents give you a place to keep your boots and gear dry without bringing muddy stuff into the tent with you. Emergency contacts are made through an iridium phone and an avionics radio. There is nothing extraneous, though. Remember, as the customer, you are ultimately paying for air-freighting that gear in to the river, and those Beavers don't come cheap.

Meals of either fresh or canned food are prepared daily. Salmon is on the menu when bright fish are available, and a Dolly or two will make the frying pan. No rainbows are killed, however, regardless of the regulations. Clients are expected to help load and unload the boats and set up their own tents. Beyond that, they can fish while dinner is being prepared—a luxury I've never had on my own float trips. Chuck runs either one or two rafts, with up to four clients. He will take a pre-arranged group of up to six if requested. Beyond those numbers, float trips just become too unwieldy. He is usually on the water for eight to ten hours a day, but only three to five hours are spent floating, with the rest of the time devoted to fishing.

The guide should provide a detailed list of recommendations on what you need to bring, in terms of both fishing tackle and personal items. Follow the list closely, and don't add extra weight and bulk. Too much clothing and superfluous electronics are the primary culprits. Tackle, clothing, bedroll, and alcohol are the primary items that the client is expected to provide. Excellent raingear is critical. Leave the cotton behind, and stick to polypro and pile. The bugs are not as bad as most people fear, but a head net weighs nothing and will give you a break from any serious infestations.

If you are considering a trip, Chuck says there are some questions you should ask before you decide on a river (most float-trip guides focus on two or three rivers and do only a few trips a season). You should find out the water depth, speed, and wadability of the river. Ask about the weather patterns, both generally and then shortly before the trip. Alaskan weather, particularly in the western part of the state, often gets into patterns that last until the jet stream moves, meaning that you may have several weeks of sun to bask in or a continuing series of Bering Sea lows to contend with. If you are concerned about bears, and most people are, ask about their concentrations, whether they are habituated to people, and what procedures are used to deter them from coming into camp.

Doing without a lodge means dealing with the weather and the bugs, but they are not really tough trips. Chuck has taken people in their seventies on these trips. The most important thing is to have the proper attitude and a good sense of humor. Float trips will give you the true Alaskan experience. Camping on a gravel bar with no one else within miles, watching an evening sunset, listening to a wolf pack howl, and eating grilled salmon—that's about as good as fishing gets.

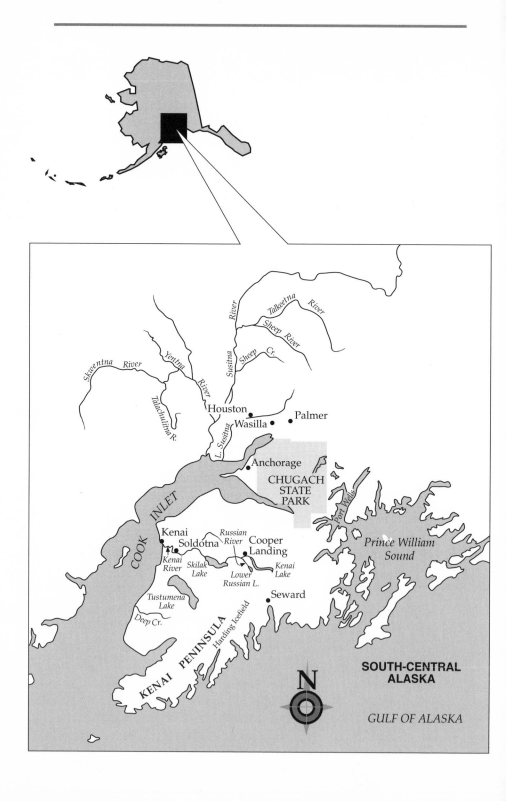

Houston
Wasilla
Palmer
Skwentna River
Yentna River
Talachulitna R.
Susitna River
Sheep River
Talkeetna River
Sheep Cr.
L. Susitna
Anchorage
CHUGACH STATE PARK
Port Wells
Prince William Sound
Kenai
Soldotna
Russian River
Cooper Landing
Kenai River
Skilak Lake
Lower Russian L.
Kenai Lake
Tustumena Lake
Seward
Deep Cr.
Harding Icefield
COOK INLET
KENAI PENINSULA
N
SOUTH-CENTRAL ALASKA
GULF OF ALASKA

PART II

SOUTH-CENTRAL ALASKA: FISHING ALONG THE ROAD SYSTEM

South-central Alaska, which encompasses the road system from the Susitna Valley through the Kenai Peninsula, is the most populated and visited part of the state. There's a good mix of trout and salmon fishing here, with all five species of salmon present. Fishing can be excellent, but the popular spots are invariably crowded when the runs are at their peak. Access is easy and campgrounds are plentiful. There are a few fly-fishing-only areas, but the most important of these, the Kenai-Russian confluence, is fly-fishing in name only, since the majority of anglers use spinning gear to lob heavy weights and crude bucktails at the hordes of salmon. Nevertheless, many of these streams are best fished with a fly, particularly for rainbows and char.

The primary target species on the Kenai River is sockeye salmon. Sockeyes arrive in the millions, but they are notoriously difficult fish to catch. Billy Coulliette and his partner, the late Curt Trout, developed techniques that will work not only in the Kenai, but in any river that sees a run of sockeyes. On the other hand, the techniques used for trout fishing on the Kenai are pretty much exclusive to that river. Bruce Nelson explains the methods he uses.

North of Anchorage, the rivers drain the slopes of the Talkeetnas and the Alaska Range. The big rivers, like the Susitna and its major tributaries, are silt choked and unfishable. But the clear-water streams that empty into them have some of the best trout and salmon fishing on the road system. Chad Valentine explains how to fish these mixed systems.

7

THE KENAI RIVER SYSTEM

In some ways the Kenai River—a brawling blue-green giant with salmon runs that lure anglers by the thousands—epitomizes the whole of Alaska. It's the most well-known and heavily used river in the state. Road-accessible throughout most of its length, the Kenai is not only a tourist destination, but also the major playground for the residents of Anchorage, Alaska's largest city. In spite of the heavy use it receives, it still carries an aura of wildness. Moose and eagles are common, and more than one startled angler has lost a stringer of fish to an opportunistic grizzly bear.

Much of the Kenai's reputation is based on its king salmon, the largest strain of salmon in the world. Bigger crowds by far, though, swarm to the river in hopes of landing a limit of sockeyes, which return every summer by the millions. In late summer, coho fishing is good. The Kenai's salmon runs provide the table fare for a huge percentage of Alaskans' summer barbecues. But for fly fishers, its trophy rainbows and abundant Dollies are an even bigger draw, filling the upper river with drift boats during the peak of the trout season in August and September.

For years, the Kenai's glacier-tinted waters were largely untouched. There was some fishing in the clear-water tributaries, where fish could be seen, but it wasn't until the middle of the last century that anglers discovered that trout and salmon could be taken in the main river. Snagging salmon was outlawed, and techniques for catching sockeyes on a fly were developed. Now newspaper headlines read, "The reds are in," and residents head to the confluence of the Russian River and the Kenai to fill their freezers.

By the late 1970s, the Kenai had also gained a reputation as a big-trout river, with a limit of one rainbow over thirty inches. The heavy fishing traffic has taken its toll, however, and although there are still some very big trout, those double-digit fish are much harder to come by in recent years. The river has always had a large population of Dollies, and that remains true. Current techniques, particularly the use of pegged beads instead of flies, have dramatically increased the catch rates on both species.

The Kenai River eases full born from the deep waters of its name-sake lake. The twenty-mile-long lake acts as huge settling pond for the tons of glacial silt that flow into it. By the time icemelt reaches the outlet, all but the finest particles have drifted to the bottom, making the river a striking aquamarine blue. Summer heat melts the glaciers, creating the anomaly of a river that rises, sometimes dramatically, during hot, dry weather. The river flows for some sixteen miles through a spruce-and birch-lined valley until it empties into Skilak Lake. At the far end of the lake, it emerges even larger, its character changed. From Skilak, it runs through a broad plain, past the town of Soldotna, and then empties into Cook Inlet, about thirty-five river miles from its source.

The lower stretch, from Soldotna to the ocean, is the favored water for those seeking the river's king salmon. These are fish that follow the deepest water in the river, and specimens approaching one hundred pounds have been hooked. It is not fly-rod country; almost all of the fishing is done with salmon eggs for bait or by pulling plugs.

The middle section, between Skilak Lake and Soldotna, has some bank fishing, and a few places directly below the lake have some very large rainbows. Realistically, only a few portions of this stretch can be fished with a fly rod, and then only when water levels have dropped. Most of the fish are tucked down in deep runs that are just too difficult to get a fly into. The entire middle and lower sections of the river see a great deal of boat traffic, particularly during the king run. Most of the fishing is done by back-trolling, and there is serious competition between the boats for the prime king slots.

It is the upper section of the river that is of interest to us here. Almost all the fly fishing on the Kenai River takes place between

Kenai Lake and Skilak Lake. The river here is big, but it has gravel bars, islands, and side channels that create holding and feeding lies. Motors are not allowed on this stretch of river, and drift boats, rafts, and individual pontoon boats ferry people from hole to hole.

The main highway runs alongside the river for most of the stretch between the Kenai Lake outlet and a boat ramp known as Jim's Landing. This stretch has good bank fishing for the walk-in angler, so a boat is not necessary, although it does allow access to islands and the opposite bank. Be aware, though, that many stretches of the banks are closed to angling. King salmon fry spend much of their life hiding in the shallow edges of the river, and bank closures are necessary in order to minimize damage to this critical habitat.

From Kenai Lake down to Skilak, the river has three distinct sections, and the fishing varies among them. Although the upper lake itself has almost no fishing, that changes dramatically right at the bridge that marks the beginning of the river. The bottom end of the lake, the hundred yards or so just above the bridge at Cooper Landing, is relatively shallow, and its slow currents allow a large number of Dollies and rainbows to cruise the water. There's usually a drift boat or two anchored up here looking for a few fish. During the late part of the season, just before freeze-up, this stretch provides the last gasp of fishing as the rainbows move back up into the lake for the winter.

The first hundred yards or so below the bridge are also worth a drift or two. The river picks up speed within a short distance, and the best fishing method is bouncing a fly along the bottom from a drifting boat. This stretch has gravel bars and a few shallow areas where you can wade and fish, but access is limited along much of it, and the brushy banks and fast, deep water prevent wading out far enough to get a clean backcast. For a wading angler, a Spey rod can open up a lot of water that most fishers cannot reach.

Although this upper stretch of river sees a fair amount of use, the Kenai comes into its own, as both a trout destination and a salmon river, about seven miles downstream, where its most famous tributary, the Russian River, joins it. During the peak of the sockeye season, known locally as the red run, the confluence attracts thousands of anglers who stand literally shoulder-to-shoulder, relentlessly flipping crude flies and heavy weights into the turbid water. A ferry moves hordes of anglers across the river—all of the fishing is on the south

side, where the Russian flows in—and returns them, frequently dragging limits of sockeyes.

The red run may be world famous, but it's a shock for fly anglers
who aren't prepared for the show. Although ostensibly a fly-fishing-only
section, the term fly fishing here is used in its loosest sense. It requires
only that a single-hook fly be used, and most of the people there don't
go beyond a crude bucktail known for some reason as a coho fly,
though no self-respecting coho would touch it. Any kind of tackle is
acceptable, and you can see everything from expensive fly rods to surf-
casting rigs.

On a given day, thousands of sockeyes will migrate up to the Russian, swimming only a few feet from shore. It may not be an aesthetic
fishery, but it's productive, and if you can make the necessary attitude
adjustment, it's a fun one. People are friendly, and although most of
them have no idea how to fish, techniques are simple and hopes are
high. The mass of anglers thins out as you walk downstream, and you
can eventually find a spot where you can cast a fly. The reward is one of
Alaska's hardest-fighting fish, and some of the best eating.

Along the Russian are a string of fish-cleaning tables that see a
steady stream of filleted carcasses pitched back into the river—feeding
stations for some very large trout. Fishing below the cleaning tables on
the Kenai and Russian with a reddish orange flesh fly is very effective
for those who want a break from salmon and don't mind the idea of
fish that have been chummed up.

The stretch of water right at the confluence of the two rivers is
designated as a sanctuary for the sockeyes, and it remains closed until
sufficient fish have entered the river to ensure adequate escapement for
spawning. In a year of good returns, though, the sanctuary opens to
angling after the first glut of fish moves through. The sharp line
between the clear water of the Russian and the glacially tinged water
of the Kenai is a magnet for migrating fish, and the sanctuary is one of
the best spots on the river to take sockeyes.

Below the Russian, the river changes. This marks the boundary
line of the Kenai National Wildlife Refuge, and the next stretch of
water is often referred to as the Refuge. This section has more islands
and back channels, and the public status of the land makes access easier.
Much of the bank is closed to fishing in order to protect the edges

used by salmon fry, but there are plenty of stretches where an angler can walk in from the road. The back channels, blown-down cottonwoods, and ledge drops provide cover for trout and char. The sockeye fishing, though not as fast as at the Russian River confluence, is productive and far less crowded. This area also has good fishing for silvers.

It is an easy day's float from the Kenai Lake bridge to Jim's Landing, but enough fishing is available to start or end the float at the Russian River boat ramp. The Kenai is not a technically difficult river to float, but it is powerful, deceptively fast, and most important, very cold. Every summer, someone dies in an accident that would have been just a discomfort on most rivers. If you fall in, you have only minutes before the cold saps your strength to the point where you will be unable to save yourself. Always wear a lifejacket on the Kenai, and pay attention to where the river is trying to take you.

Below Jim's Landing, the river drops through a steep-walled canyon. This stretch has only limited areas of holding water and a couple of class-three rapids that need to be negotiated. The biggest obstacle to floating this stretch is the long trip across Skilak Lake to reach the nearest boat ramp.

The canyon has very little walk-in access, except at the bottom where the river dumps into Skilak Lake. Good fishing can be had there, particularly in the late fall and early spring. The rainbows drop down out of the river once the autumn bounty of food has been washed out. Many of the old salmon carcasses settle into this first section of the lake, and a pretty good crowd of nice rainbows can be found there. The river mouth can be reached by boat from the Skilak campgrounds and is therefore crowded at times. For those considering crossing Skilak, either at the end of a float trip through the canyon or to explore the fishing at the mouth, be aware that it is a very dangerous body of water. The lake is close to the weather-producing glaciers of the Harding Icefield. Winds can come up suddenly, and its shallow waters can quickly develop a nasty chop.

As with all Alaska fishing, the first criterion for success on the Kenai is timing. The season opens on June 11, just as the first run of sockeyes appears. The early season usually sees a bit of good fishing for rainbows, but the number of salmon fishers can be intimidating. Fortunately, the trout tend to prefer different habitat than the salmon use for their migration—and whether they prefer it or not, the sockeyes simply push them out of the migration lanes. The first of the Kenai's two runs of sockeyes ends about July 10. These early fish all go up the Russian River and into its upper headwaters to spawn. The second, larger run hits the upper river about July 20. These fish spawn in the Kenai itself, as well as the Russian and other tributaries.

There's usually a period of a week or so between runs when you see essentially no sockeye in the river—and a lot of uninformed and disappointed anglers. This slack period is a good opportunity to try for midseason trout. Although no eggs are in the river at this time, egg patterns are always effective, but sculpins, leeches, or beadhead nymphs more closely match the food on which the rainbows are feeding. A bit of dry-fly fishing is available on the Russian River during this period, although the bigger fish will still be holding in the Kenai.

The king salmon also have two runs, and although fishing for them is not allowed in the upper river, their presence has a profound impact on the rainbows. Once the kings start to spawn, the trout will abandon their protected lies close to shore and move out into the heavier water preferred by the spawning chinooks. The first run of kings begins to trickle in before the season opens, and the second shows up in mid-July. They start to pair up and dig their redds about mid-August.

The Kenai also has good fishing for silver salmon, with the first run beginning in late July and peaking in mid-August. A second run hits the river in September, ensuring that some salmon are available until the end of the season. This is perhaps the most important coho fishery in the state, and although it is always crowded, it provides ample opportunities to take a silver on a fly rod. Just don't go undergunned; a fresh coho in a river as big and powerful as the Kenai will tear you up.

The rainbows and char, whose survival is tied to the salmon cycles, are also seasonal, although somewhat less so than in other large rivers. They feed on sculpins and insects during the early part of the season, but as the salmon move in, they migrate upstream with them. The best fishing for trout comes in late summer and early fall, when they stack up behind the spawning salmon, concentrating on the eggs. Because the Kenai hosts both kings and sockeyes, the trout have a longer period to feed than those fish that live in systems that are home to only a single predominant species. By mid-September, the kings have started to die, and their carcasses hang up on snags and in eddies. The trout begin to lose their fixation on eggs, and flesh flies, sculpins, and leeches will take fish.

The Kenai's most important tributary, the Russian River, is the antithesis of the Kenai—a small, clear freestone stream, perfect for sight fishing and short casts. In spite of its size, it is one of the keys to the larger river's reputation as a fishing destination. Like the Kenai, it is a two-lake system, beginning in Upper Russian Lake, flowing eight miles to Lower Russian Lake, and then tumbling through a canyon, past a campground full of avid anglers, to its confluence with the Kenai.

The Russian's reputation is based on the two runs of sockeyes that use this system. The first run of Kenai reds spawns exclusively in the upper Russian system, filling the river with schools of bright salmon for a couple weeks, and then climbing the Russian Falls and leaving the lower river empty. The second run uses the entire Kenai system, but many of these fish spawn in the Russian, providing food for the trout and char that follow them into the river.

Sockeye fishing can be very good in the Russian, but the clear water makes it a bit more challenging than the Kenai. This is not a bad thing, though, because it means that there are far fewer anglers competing for the prime runs. Fewer is relative, however, and the Russian is still crowded when the reds are in. As is always the case with sockeyes, the fishing is best in water that is moving. In spite of its steep gradient and overall speed, the Russian has a few deep, slow pools, and the big schools of fish in them attract a lot of anglers. Although you see some hookups there, most of the fish that come from these pools are snagged. Those who swing a fly across the knee-deep water with constant current will almost always do better. Paradoxically, fewer people fish this type of water. Once the salmon arrive on their spawning beds and turn color, they are useless for sport or food and should be left to spawn in peace.

Although both salmon and trout can be found throughout the system, most of the fishing is concentrated in the stretch of water from the campground downstream to the confluence. There are pools and runs that hold salmon as they pass through, and the gravel-bottomed salmon spawning grounds draw trout and char. Both smolt and fry migrate out of the Russian, and some early-season fishing is available. The prime fishing is after the reds have started to spawn. Look for fish behind the spawning sockeyes. The dark backs of the rainbows can be spotted, but it's difficult to see Dollies in the water. Sockeyes are very aggressive when they start to pair up, and they chase the trout mercilessly. If the salmon are pairing up and you see no trout, move down to the confluence where trout will hold, waiting for the salmon to begin spawning. A few intrepid rainbows, usually smaller fish, can be found in the faster water below the spawning runs. With no eggs in the water, trout will be feeding on the nymphs stirred up by the redd-building. Prince Nymphs, Hare's Ears, and Pheasant Tails all work well. Once the salmon begin to spawn in earnest, the trout and Dollies become selective to eggs, and although it's still possible to fool some large, difficult trout with a carefully presented nymph, egg patterns are "match-the-hatch" trout food.

Fishing with beads is currently illegal in fly-fishing-only waters in south-central Alaska, and that includes the Russian River before late August (check the exact date in the regulations). But Glo-Bugs and other egg flies still catch fish. You just need to become more adept at detecting a strike. Don't expect any late-season fishing here; the trout and char don't overwinter in the Russian, and they disappear as soon as the first big autumn rain washes out the carcasses they were feeding on.

For anglers who want to avoid the late season crowds on the Russian, Quartz Creek is a good alternative. It has very few rainbows, but a healthy population of Dollies moves in during August, and some of them are very large. Although they are in the creek preparing for their own spawning season, they are also fattening up on eggs and flesh. Here you'll have willing fish, beautiful clear water, and most of the runs to yourself.

Techniques for trout and char on the Russian River and Quartz Creek are essentially identical to those used on other sockeye streams; refer to the extensive advice provided by Jack and John Holman in the Bristol Bay chapter.

The Kenai River has a lot of guides, and some are very good. Most of them concentrate on king salmon until August 1, and remain in the lower river, turning to trout once the salmon spawning starts. Only a few of them are fly-rod specialists, and among the best are Bruce Nelson of Cooper Landing and Billy Coulliette and the late Curt Trout, owners of the aptly named Troutfitters. Their advice will give you a solid base for pursuing salmon, trout, and char on Alaska's most popular river.

8

TROUT FISHING ON THE KENAI
with Bruce Nelson

It was 7:30 on a brisk morning in mid-September when I walked down the boat ramp at the Cooper Landing Bridge. The sun was just burning through a thick mist, giving the sky an incandescent glow. A drift boat, with fly rods jutting over the gunwales, was silhouetted alongside the bridge abutments. I could just make out a single figure leaning over the boat. "Morning, Bruce," I said.

Bruce Nelson has been guiding trout fishers on the Kenai since the mid-1970s and has a well-deserved reputation as one of the river's top-notch guides. Thin and wiry, he has the air of a man at ease with his lifestyle. He lives on the river and has two kids, both of whom love to fish. A significant limp doesn't slow him down.

"Climb in," he said, pushing the twenty-foot drift boat over to the shore. "We'll try this stretch of slow water just above the bridge. There are a lot of trout and Dollies that hold in here. What weight rod did you bring?"

Bruce likes to fish with 5- or 6-weights, depending on the amount of lead needed to get down to the fish. All of the fishing is done with floating lines, which lets the thin monofilament leader slice through the Kenai's turbulent currents. He rigged me up with a 9-foot leader, ending in 14-pound fluorocarbon tippet. "We get a big volume of fish, and I like to use tippet heavy enough to keep fishing without spending a lot of time changing tackle. Those rocks on the bottom fray a leader pretty quickly if you're fishing right."

Bruce's rigging technique was not one that I had seen before. He puts a loop in the end of the leader, leaving a long tag, in which he ties a stopper knot. He pinches one or two split shot onto the tag and attaches the tippet with a loop-to-loop connection. "The weight is critical," he explains. "You should be able to feel the split shot just ticking the bottom but not slowing the drift down."

Unlike most Kenai River fishers, Bruce does not use a strike indicator, relying on a tight line to detect the fish. "A strike indicator works well only if the depth is constant and you have it properly adjusted. With the variations in current and depth that we see, you would have to change the positioning of the indicator on almost every cast."

Like every guide on the river, Bruce uses pegged beads instead of flies. The use of beads has dramatically changed the success rate on the Kenai. The trout and Dollies feed almost exclusively on eggs from the time the kings begin to spawn in late July until the sockeyes finish in late September. The eggs bounce along the bottom, and a successful imitation needs to have a dead drift. The trout know that they don't have to chase down or kill an egg, and consequently the takes are very soft. Because the river is big and turbulent, it is difficult to maintain a properly drifting fly and still be able to detect a strike. Pegging the bead prevents the fish from rejecting it before the hook can be set.

Bead size can be important. King salmon eggs are best imitated with 10-millimeter beads and sockeye eggs with 6- to 8-millimeter beads. Salmon eggs change color over time, ranging from the bright pinkish orange of fresh spawn to the matte cream color of old infertile eggs. Because there are so many stages of eggs in the river at any given time, Bruce doesn't believe that color makes a lot of difference, provided that it's a good imitation of at least some of the eggs in the water. Any individual fish may be selective to a specific color, he says, but since so many fish see the bead, there are always some fish looking for that stage of egg. The possible exception is late fall, when the vast majority of eggs are old and pale. As with his refusal to use strike indicators, Bruce is a bit of an iconoclast in his ideas of bead color. Some guides, such as Curt Trout, go to incredible lengths to create a perfect match for each stage of egg development.

The color of the bead may not be important, but Bruce believes two other parts of the rig are vital to success. He has gone exclusively

to circle hooks, which improve the hookup percentage, particularly
when the angler doesn't feel the take. The most critical part, though, is
getting the weight right. This means changing the size or number of
split shot depending on water depth, current, and fishing position.
Keeping the fly at the right depth requires a willingness to constantly
adjust the amount of lead.

Once Bruce had me properly rigged, he pulled the drift boat out
to a spot just above the bridge. The current here, at the outlet of Kenai
Lake, is slow, and the fish tend to cruise. We dropped anchor and began
casting up into the lake. We let the eggs bounce through a slight
trench, picking up a few Dollies. Periodically, Bruce raised the anchor
and we drifted downstream a hundred yards or so, just to the point
where the river started to capture the boat. Bruce rowed back up and
repeated the drift several times, carefully checking to make sure that I
was still just ticking the bottom with the split shot.

We caught mostly Dollies, with an occasional rainbow. That seems
to be the usual ratio on the Kenai. The river holds both rainbows and
resident char, which winter over in the lakes and deep holes. A run of
anadromous Dollies shows up in late summer. Unlike salmon, these fish
have no set migration pattern. Kenai Dollies have been caught in Deep
Creek only a few months after being tagged.

The Kenai was once famous for the number of very large trout it
held. Fish over thirty inches were caught with some regularity. Bruce's
biggest rainbow weighed sixteen pounds, and he has taken a thirty-
incher that weighed fourteen, a very fat trout. The Dollies grow big,
too—Bruce's largest weighed thirteen pounds. With increased fishing
pressure, fish of this size have become increasingly scarce. Still, during
the peak of the season, on any given day, someone in the boat usually
ties into a fish that will go twenty-four or maybe as much as twenty-
seven inches.

Bruce and I spent most of the day fishing from the boat, bouncing
the beads along the bottom. The current is much too fast to get a second drift through a run, so you need to make your one shot at it
count. This means, above all, getting the weight right. If I wasn't touch-
ing bottom, Bruce was quick to add another split shot. If you are just
ticking the bottom, which is where you want to be, you will lose a few
flies on the rocks and snags. Bruce kept a second rod ready to go so

that I didn't miss productive water during the time it would have taken to rerig.

Bruce maneuvered the boat over likely looking runs, but the truth is that the fish are scattered throughout the river. King salmon prefer heavier water as spawning habitat, so the fishing is best in midriver during August, when they are spawning. As the sockeyes begin to contribute to the bounty of eggs, the trout follow them into the shallower water, where the bottom is made up of gravel finer than that used by the kings. Because the Kenai is glacier fed, the cooler weather of late autumn usually means low water, exposing more of the gravel bars. Carefully fishing the edges of the gravel bars is usually quite productive and is the technique of choice for walk-in anglers.

We found several runs that were more easily fished on foot, and we worked a couple of gravel bars. Bruce made sure that I started fishing very close to shore, without getting into the river until I had fished the edges carefully. The trout and Dollies will hold in very skinny water if they haven't been disturbed. I asked about switching to a flesh fly, but Bruce told me it was still a bit early in the season.

As September turns to October, the multitude of eggs begins to dwindle, and the trout and Dollies turn their attention to the carcasses of spawned-out salmon that line the banks and fill the bottom of every depression in the river. Rocks and snags collect the bodies, and as they break up, chunks of meat roll down with the current. Flesh flies become an important alternative to eggs, and the techniques begin to change. Bruce told me that the high water that follows the heavy autumn rains actually improves the fishing by getting the fish looking for flesh flies and streamers. He suggests that you work the water carefully with a dead-drifted flesh fly, but let it hang for a moment in the current at the end of the drift. Trout will often follow a fly and hit it on the hang. If you happen to be picking up to cast, you will usually either break the fish off or pull the fly from its mouth.

The typical flesh fly used by most fly fishers is a white or ginger Bunny Fly, often with a touch of pink, tied on a size 4 or 6 hook. These are effective, but they provide a big meal for fish that are often already satiated from the amount of food in the water. Bruce, like many late-fall fishers, prefers a smaller fly. His is a simple yarn pattern tied on a size 10 hook. Maggot Flies can also be productive, particularly after a fall rain. Bruce says that the little crappie grubs are his favorite imitation.

Good fishing continues well into October, but once the food sources disappear, the trout move out quickly. A heavy rain that flushes away the carcasses and loose eggs usually spells the end of drift fishing. The trout still congregate at the outlet of Kenai Lake and the upper end of Skilak Lake, though, so hard-core anglers can find fish for as long as the water remains unfrozen. By December, even the most fanatic fly fisher is looking toward spring.

Although August and September are the prime months for trout, fish are available earlier in the summer. Contrary to popular wisdom, trout fishing continues even after the sockeyes begin their run. During early summer, the trout are looking for fry that are hatching and migrating down into Skilak Lake. Bruce's favorite imitation is a traditional Muddler Minnow about an inch long, tied on a size 10 circle hook. He fishes it with a downstream belly in the line and twitches it off the bottom as it comes around on the swing. Nymphs, such as a Gold-Ribbed Hare's Ear, are also effective.

Unlike most Alaskan rivers, here the traditional leeches and Woolly Buggers are inconsistent fish catchers. However, flesh flies work surprisingly well during the early part of the season. Salmon, particularly cohos, spawn in the Kenai until midwinter, so there are always a few carcasses washed into the water by the higher flows of summer. With no eggs in the water, it can be difficult to locate trout during the first part of the season. Look for fish in the seams and slots early, but as the sockeyes move in, they will push the trout in closer to the bank—inside the moving stream of migrating salmon—or outside into heavier water.

Once the sockeyes arrive in force, most of the activity on the river turns to salmon fishing. As the season progresses, thousands of filleted carcasses are thrown into the river, particularly just below the Russian River confluence. Some very big trout live in that stretch, and most of them get fat on the chunks of bright orange sockeye flesh rolling down the bottom along either bank. An appropriate-colored flesh pattern will pull up some nice bows from the midst of the salmon fishers. The warm days of summer mean melting glaciers and heavier flow in the Kenai. The higher water actually helps the trout fishing, providing them more places to hold without being displaced by the aggressive salmon.

As you float downstream from the lake, the river gradually picks up speed, and the fishing is largely a matter of keeping the bead bouncing along the bottom. There are a few obvious slots and runs, but you need to set up for them far enough in advance to make sure that you have the fly at the proper depth. Most of the fishing is from the boat. This upper stretch of the river ends at the confluence with the Russian River, which marks the boundary of the Kenai National Wildlife Refuge.

The Refuge section, as it is called, runs from the Russian River down to the boat takeout at Jim's Landing, just above the canyon. Bruce says that under most conditions, this is the most productive stretch of the river, with lots of gravel bars and spawning beds. There is less drifting and more fishing from the bars here, and the river holds some big trout and abundant Dollies.

Although the Refuge section is usually the most productive, water levels were very low when I floated the river with Bruce. The limited water was clogged with a massive return of sockeyes, and the combination of an overabundant food source and the aggressive male sockeyes keep the well-fed trout hunkered down in holding lies. With the tough conditions, we limited our fishing to the upper stretch, above the Russian River confluence.

A little after noon, Bruce pulled into a small, boulder-bottomed bay. "If the water were a bit higher, this would almost certainly hold silvers," he said. "They like these back channels where they can get out of the current."

There were no silvers, but it made a good spot for lunch. Over sandwiches, I asked Bruce to identify the most common mistakes anglers make when fishing the Kenai. "They fish too fast. People get so psyched up about the possibility of catching a big fish that they don't work the water with the care it requires. There are a lot of fish in this river, and they hold almost everywhere. There is plenty of food, and generally, they are not going to move very far to take a fly.

"Families are really the easiest to guide. They are just interested in having fun, and they tend to listen to instruction. A lot of experienced fishers want to use the same techniques that work on their home waters, and they are not necessarily effective on this river."

According to Bruce, the key to fishing from the bank is to start in very close. "The fish will hold in very shallow water. Don't get in the water until you have fished the shoreline thoroughly. Move through the run slowly, and if it's good-looking water or you hit some fish, go back for a second pass."

As Bruce pulled the drift boat toward the boat ramp and his waiting trailer, I made one last cast, the bead sliding down an obvious seam. I mended once to keep the fly drifting at the proper depth, and the line came up tight on a nice fish. It wasn't the twenty-four-incher I'd been hoping for, but it was the best fish of the day and a fine way to end the trip.

9

SALMON SECRETS:
A Day on the Kenai with Curt Trout and Billy Coulliette

Over the past decade or so, the Kenai River has become a destination trout fishery. But its reputation and the quality of its trout fishing are based on its spectacular salmon runs. Salmon fishing on the Kenai bears no resemblance to the rarefied traditions of fishing for Atlantic salmon. This is a pure whack 'em and stack 'em meat fishery, and not even the most ardent catch-and-release trout fisher can resist the taste of a fresh sockeye fillet grilled over the coals. And with millions of fish returning every year, this is a guilt-free meal.

Most of the serious anglers on the Kenai have dropped into Trout-fitters' Fly Shop at some point. Started in 1993 by Curt Trout, Troutfit-ters provides good advice and guided trips for trout and salmon. Curt, who passed away shortly after this trip, was retiring and longtime guide Billy Coulliette was taking over his business when I was lucky enough to spend a day on the Kenai with both of them, discussing the secrets of catching sockeye and coho salmon.

It was a crisp, clear day in early April, well before the salmon—and the crowds of salmon fishers—would show up. We had the river pretty much to ourselves, with only three or four other boats venturing out. April is slow fishing here, but a few big rainbows can be found. The Kenai is glacier fed, which means that in early spring, before the glaciers begin to dump their silt load, it is low and relatively clear. Even though it was spring, Curt was fishing beads. The last of the previous summer's cohos were just dying, and a few eggs were still available for the trout. I opted for an alevin pattern, anticipating the start of the next cycle. Although we were fishing for trout, I was there to learn how to catch salmon.

The Kenai's king salmon are the largest in the world and get a lot of publicity, but it is the sockeyes that fuel the system and take most of the fishing pressure. Although sockeyes are notoriously close-mouthed, the millions that return to the Kenai every year mean that they are readily accessible to anyone who wants to take on a seven- or eight-pound sea-run fish in heavy water. The result is the most heavily used fishery in the state—a line of anglers that stretches shoulder-to-shoulder for a quarter mile downstream from the confluence of the Russian and Kenai Rivers.

The area below the confluence is designated fly-fishing-only, but it's unlike any fly fishing that occurs elsewhere. The rig of choice for many people is a surf-casting rod with 40-pound-test line, half an ounce of lead, and an unweighted bucktail tied on a hook with a gap of less than $3/8$ inch. The fly itself is all that's required to meet the fly-fishing-only designation.

In spite of the assortment of gear that can be found, a lot of fish are caught on traditional fly-fishing tackle, even if the techniques are somewhat unique. Billy likes an 8- or 9-weight rod, as it's simply too easy to break a smaller rod on these fish. He says that sockeyes account for more broken rods than any other species. Billy also prefers a long rod. With his technique, a 10-footer makes it easier to control the drift and ensure that the fly is down to the fish's depth during the sweet part of the swing. Although a sinking-tip can be effective in the right hands, most anglers simply use a floating line. For the client's rigs, Troutfitters uses double-tapers and cuts them in half. You definitely don't need to worry about long casts with these fish.

The Kenai has two runs of sockeyes. The first has already started to enter the river when the season opens on June 11, although the bulk of the fish may not be past Skilak Lake at that time. That run lasts until about July 10. The second run enters the river a week or so later and is in the upper river by July 20. Most of the fishing for reds is done in the upper river, particularly at the mouth of the Russian. Some very good fishing can be had below Skilak Lake, however, particularly on the second run. The river bottom here has more pea gravel and fewer boulders, so it is more amenable to drifting a fly at the proper depth without hanging up. The fish in this section are chrome bright and still carry a load of sea lice. They move fast through here, though, so the river empties out in about two weeks.

Successful sockeye fishing requires that the fish be moving. It's almost impossible to resist casting to salmon that are stacked up and rolling in slow water, but it's a futile gesture. Although they are almost impossible to catch, Billy likes to see large groups of fish in the slack water. According to him, the best fishing is found in the fast shallows just above the holding water. As more fish move into the hole, they tend to push the uppermost fish out and into water where they are vulnerable to a properly swung fly. In the right place, you will have a steady supply of fish moving past your fly, and with sockeyes, numbers are important.

Sockeyes travel close to the bottom and will not move up for a fly. Much of the Kenai is full of boulders and rubble, making hangups and gear replacement a constant problem. The best areas are those with a pea gravel bottom—the stuff typically found at the lower end of the gravel bars. Adjust your weight to match the depth and speed of the water.

A number of techniques are used for sockeyes in the Kenai, but the successful ones have a common theme. They take advantage of a some-what dismaying, but undoubtedly true fact about catching reds: These fish rarely take a fly. They live on plankton and krill in the ocean and have no search image or mental trigger that causes them to grab a fly during their migration. Sockeyes that are colored up and on the redds, on the other hand, are very aggressive and will hit anything. However, they are worthless as a food fish, are not much sport, and should not be disturbed when spawning. Almost all of the sockeyes taken in the Kenai are caught because the leader drifts into a fish's open mouth and the fly pulls into the outer jaw. The fish are essentially snagged in the mouth.

The name of the game is to avoid snagging them in the back, tail, or any area other than the head. A foul-hooked sockeye in the Kenai's heavy current puts breaking-strength strain on your rod and gear, takes forever to land, and must be released. Many of the techniques seen on the river result in multiple foul hookups for every legal fish landed. The technique used by Curt and Billy is designed to minimize that problem.

They use 30-pound-test as a butt section for their leaders. The weight is attached to the end of that section. The tippet is 20-pound-test, from 4 to 6 feet long. These fish are not leader shy, and you need to put some pressure on them if they get out into the river, so heavy tippet is standard. The leader distance is critical. The length of tippet is dependent on water speed, with 4 feet being about right for fast water and up to 6 feet if the water is slower. State regulations require that the weight be at least eighteen inches above the fly. By going with a much longer distance, this technique minimizes the problem with foul hooking. A leader that hangs up on the fish's tail or dorsal fin will slide off before the hook is dragged into the fish.

The fly must be right at the fish's depth. This means using enough weight that the fly just taps along the bottom. Too much weight and you will hang on the bottom, which not only can cost you a new rig, but also swings the fly dead downstream from the weight, almost eliminating the possibility of a hookup.

One of the most common—and most critical—mistakes made by anglers is wading deep. Sockeyes, unlike kings, run along the shore. They will migrate in just a couple feet of water, particularly in off-color rivers like the Kenai. Those fishers who wade out thigh-deep simply push the fish farther offshore, into deeper water, where it's much more difficult to keep your fly in the zone during the swing. The plunk of heavy lead splashing into the water will also move fish out of their preferred route, so some delicacy, though not easy with the weight required, is helpful.

Billy and I took time off from our April trout fishing so he could demonstrate his technique for getting a proper drift. He describes it as a three-step process designed to keep the fly in the fish's zone for the maximum time. "The first step is to cast straight across the river—a twelve o'clock cast. It's easiest if you pick a marker on the opposite side, not upstream or down, and consistently cast toward it. The line, leader, and fly need to be in a straight line. These are just short casts. Ten or fifteen feet is about right. You may need to lengthen it to reach the fish if other anglers downstream from you have waded too deep and moved the fish out from the bank."

Because of the short cast and heavy weight, a traditional overhead cast is neither necessary nor useful. It can also be dangerous. Simply lift the line so that the weight is at the surface of the water, and then flip it directly out in front of you.

The second step is to drop the rod tip into the water. This allows the line to remain deep and at the proper angle relative to the current. You need to have sufficient weight to get the fly to the bottom almost immediately—another reason to fish in shallower water.

The final trick is to keep the rod tip moving ahead of the line as it drifts downstream. This will avoid creating a belly in the line and keep everything straight. "If you keep your arm straight, with no bend in the elbow, it will force you to use the proper technique," Billy says.

Strikes will come as the fly hits the ten o'clock position, about forty-five degrees downstream. Once the fly gets past that point, pick it up and flip it back to twelve o'clock. Don't bother letting the fly hang below you as you would for trout. Also don't bother casting to fish that you see upstream from you. Once they get out of that zone directly in front of you, a good drift is impossible, and you should concentrate on the fish that are still coming, not the ones that have already gone.

Sockeye takes are very soft—no more than the fly stopping in the water. It can be very helpful if you pick a single spot and make consistent, rhythmic casts. As you become accustomed to the feel of the fly bouncing along the bottom, you become more attuned to the anomalous bumps that signal a fish.

The strikes may be gentle, but there's nothing subtle about the way a sockeye fights once it feels the hook. They will usually make a long run downstream, interspersed with cartwheeling jumps. You can't always follow the fish, and dragging an angry seven- or eight-pound salmon back upstream in a river as big as the Kenai can be problematic at best. Curt developed a little trick that saved the day with a number of big fish that had gotten downstream of him. Put the rod tip in the water, pointing directly at the fish, and take most of the pressure off. The fish will get back in line and start to move upstream again. By using light, steady pressure and not panicking the fish, you can reel them right up to the rod tip—but watch out then. Alternatively, you can use the same technique to hold the fish in position while you scramble downstream to fight it, or take the pressure off completely and the fish will eventually swim right back upstream to you.

I have left sockeye flies for last, simply because they are the least important aspect of the gear on the Kenai. Fish are caught on everything from big bucktails to sparse Comets. The usual caveat of using smaller sparse flies may still hold here, but it's less important. The economics of the guiding business mean that Curt and Billy were happy to get away with a simple dark yarn fly, little more than a bit of Glo-Bug yarn in black or dark green, either tied to the hook or fastened with an egg loop and cut about an inch long. Some anglers like to use a reddish orange Bunny Fly that imitates chunks of fresh sockeye flesh. Some large trout or Dollies are often hanging along the edge of the migrating salmon, and they are getting fat on the scraps of filleted sockeyes.

Just make sure that the hook is legal—no more than a $^3/_8$-inch gap and unweighted. And assuming that you plan to keep the fish, do not pinch down the barb. Because most of the hookups are on the opposite side of the mouth, a barbless hook will pop out when the fish starts to turn and fight.

Sockeyes and kings get all the publicity on the Kenai, but a good run of silvers comes through in late summer. Cohos enter the river in late August, with the peak of the season in September through mid-October. They are in many ways the antithesis of sockeyes. They are aggressive to the fly, very spooky, and capable of being extremely picky about the fly they will hit.

Billy likes an 8-weight outfit for silvers, as did Curt, although you can get away with a 7-weight. Although some fishers prefer a sinking-tip line for these fish, a floating line is enough for these depths. Silvers will shy away from a line flashing in the air, so dark lines are preferable to brightly colored ones. A level 20-pound-test leader is best. Silvers are surprisingly fragile fish, and if you plan to release them unharmed, it's important to get them in while they are hot, before they build up a deadly load of lactic acid.

These are fickle fish, and a wide variety of flies can be important. Glo-Bugs, Muddler Minnows, and leeches all take silvers, particularly in shallow water. If they don't hit a fly within the first cast or two, they probably want something different, in terms of either the fly or the retrieve. Billy has developed an efficient system for approaching each pod of fish. He starts with a small, dark fly, often a Starlight Leech. He makes his first cast to the outside of the school and tries a very slow retrieve. If that doesn't elicit any interest, he tries the same fly with a faster retrieve. The next step is to switch to a brighter or flashier fly and go through the same retrieve sequence.

Billy says that there are also times when a small, size 6 or 8 black beadhead Woolly Bugger works well. The critical thing with cohos in the Kenai, as elsewhere, is to keep experimenting until you find something that works, and when it quits working, try something different. One thing that doesn't seem to work on the Kenai is skated dry flies. While it may be possible to get a fish to chase a Pink Pollywog in the right water, it is much less productive here than on many other rivers.

Most of the flies are size 2, but smaller ones are sometimes necessary. For brighter colors, Billy likes fuchsia flies, tied with bunny fur or marabou, or the classic Flash Fly, tied with Flashabou and red hackle. One of the most productive flies is a black Articulated Leech with a flame head and some Flashabou.

Unlike sockeye fishing, the most productive water for silvers is the slow eddies and back sloughs where the fish have stacked up. These conditions seem to make them more aggressive and likely to hit a fly. Some of the best fishing occurs when heavy autumn rains bring very high water. It creates lots of back sloughs that attract fish and at the same time drives the trout fishers off the water, leaving the river empty of competition. The best fishing is in the upper river, although the middle river can also be good.

Approach cohos carefully and remain out of sight. By taking fish from the edge of the school and working them quickly into the current, away from the rest of the fish, you may get as many as three fish from a school before they shut down. As is usual with silvers, the best fishing is at first light in the morning, before the sun is on the water. It's also helpful to be the first boat to hit a school, before other anglers have put the fish down. Needless to say, even in September's shorter days, this means an early start on the river.

Although the Kenai is famous for having the largest king salmon in the world, they are almost impossible to take on a fly rod. They prefer the heavy, deep water of the main channel, where it's very difficult to get a fly to their depth. But if you want the challenge of a big gamefish in fresh water, take your 12-weight and some big flies to the middle river, from the Moose River down, and try late in the evening, when the kings will occasionally move into shallower water. It's not consistent, but who knows, you may tie into the next tippet class record.

For the casual Alaskan visitor, fishing in Alaska is defined by catching sockeye on the Kenai. It is productive, the results are delicious, and it requires little in the way of expertise and tackle. But even hard-core local fly fishers make the pilgrimage when the reds are in, usually at the urging of a family member who has had enough of catch-and-release and wants some edible results from all those lost weekends. And when the opportunity came to put Billy and Curt's techniques into practice, I made sure that there was plenty of charcoal on hand for the results.

10

SUSITNA VALLEY

North of Anchorage, a massive watershed drains the southern slopes of the Alaska Range, emptying centuries-old glacial melt into Cook Inlet. Flowing down its namesake valley, the Susitna River is huge and turbid, full of sweepers and mudbanks, and completely unsuitable for casting a fly. Similar, somewhat smaller tributaries, like the Talkeetna and Skwentna, flow through the rolling hills and birch forests of the valley, adding their loads of silt to the main river. But the small-clear water streams that join them provide some of the best fishing in south-central Alaska. They get wonderful runs of king salmon and cohos; hold rainbows, char, and grayling; and provide food and sport for many of the people living in Anchorage and points north.

Mention fishing in "the Valley" to most Alaskans, and their thoughts will focus on a series of streams that cross the Parks Highway, a transportation corridor that runs north from the strip-mall town of Wasilla past Denali National Park. These include the Little Susitna River and Willow, Sheep, and Montana Creeks. But the Susitna drains a huge area with other, more interesting, if less accessible streams. Jet boats roar up the Talkeetna, ferrying anglers to the mouths of wilderness waterways. On the west side of the Susitna, Lake Creek and the Deshka and Talachulitna Rivers beckon. The intimate size and easy accessibility of most of these streams make for fisheries that are open to anyone who wants to try—guides and boats are not required.

The roadside streams provide an everyman experience. Easily accessible and managed for the maximum harvest of salmon, they have a combat-fishing atmosphere when the kings and silvers are running, but they are small enough to be waded and easily fished with a fly rod. Don't expect the rarefied atmosphere of the Battenkill here. Kids, dogs, and grandmothers all join in the fun. Beer, loud music, and large-caliber sidearms are much more common than fly-tying vises or single-malt scotch. But there are lots of fish, and as long as you are willing to accept the campground crowds on their own terms, you will have as much fun as they are obviously having.

Most of the fishing on these streams occurs from the highway crossing downstream to the Susitna. Upstream from the Parks Highway, the crowds thin out dramatically, and there is good fishing for grayling, char, and rainbows. Check the regulations, though. On many streams, salmon fishing is prohibited upstream from the highway to protect the spawning fish. All of the rivers in the Susitna drainage are susceptible to being blown out by heavy rains, pretty much an annual occurrence. Some are worse than others, but most clear up fairly quickly once the storms have passed through.

The most popular streams are the Little Susitna River and Willow Creek. The Little Su flows from its headwaters in the Talkeetnas into Cook Inlet. It gets a good run of kings, but its reputation was made on its coho fishery. There are about twenty miles of easily floatable river between the town of Houston and its road-accessible confluence with the Susitna at Burma Landing. Much of the lower river is more easily fished by boat, and the quality of the fishing is dependent on the tides. A bit farther up, the river narrows and is more suitable for a fly rod.

Willow Creek is a small, clear-water stream that can provide great fishing and often has shoulder-to-shoulder crowds. It is possible to wade the entire stretch of the river from the highway crossing to its confluence with the Susitna, a distance of about four miles. A large campground is situated near the mouth, and many people use canoes to float this stretch. Willow gets one of the best runs of king salmon of any road-accessible river in the state. It also has good fishing for silvers in August. Upstream from the highway, Hatcher Pass Road follows the river valley and provides access to some late-season fishing for grayling and rainbows.

Farther up the Parks Highway, Montana and Sheep Creeks also provide good fishing, although Sheep Creek is not very fly-rod friendly. Both streams get good returns of kings and see significant

crowds during late June and early July. Montana Creek is less susceptible than some of the other rivers in the area to being blown out by
rain or snowmelt. Its small size makes it a good fly-fishing stream.
Montana Creek's confluence with the Susitna is an easy walk from the
highway, so it gets a lot of attention. You'll also find some good fishing
for rainbows upstream from the highway.

For those with a few more dollars and a desire for less raucous set-
tings, there are some top-notch fly-out streams in this huge drainage.
Most of these rivers have lodges at their mouths. Some make good
float trips for the experienced rafter who wants a wilderness experience without the cost of flying to western Alaska.

The Talachulitna, the area's premier float, is a beautiful river. Starting at Judd Lake, it flows placidly past rolling hills to the midpoint,
then drops through steep-walled canyons, boiling into some impressive
class-three rapids. The Tal gets good runs of chinooks and silvers, and
with the imposition of mandatory release of rainbows, it has come
back as a first-class trout stream. The lower part of the river has excep-
tional fishing. The Tal resembles the streams of southwest Alaska, and
the techniques used by Jack Holman and Chuck Ash will stand you in
good stead if you are planning to fish it.

Lake Creek is another wilderness destination easily accessible from
Anchorage. It is crowded at the mouth when the kings arrive during
June and early July, but float trips are productive. The creek begins at
the foot of Mount McKinley and flows south to its confluence with
the Yentna. Like the Tal, it has some serious whitewater and is not a
river for the inexperienced rafter. It has good fishing for all five species
of salmon and some nice resident rainbows.

One of the nicest rivers, the Deshka, gets good runs of kings and
has excellent fishing for rainbows in the upper stretch. It's a worry-free
float through spruce and birch forest. Unfortunately, it's accessible by
jet boat from the Parks Highway and consequently sees a lot of anglers.
Once the king season ends, the boat traffic slows dramatically, and the
rainbows can be found behind spawning salmon.

The third way to fish the Susitna drainage is to take a riverboat up
the Talkeetna and fish the clear-water streams that flow into it. This is a
river for experienced boaters only. The town of Talkeetna, the jumping-
off point for climbers headed to Mount McKinley, has several outfitters
who will run anglers upstream as drop-offs or on guided trips.

Clear Creek is the best known of the Talkeetna tributaries, and during the king season, its banks can resemble the campgrounds at the roadside streams. Several other creeks have comparable fishing, however. There is a short period of good trout fishing in May, before the spring runoff hits. During this early part of the season, the trout are stacked up at the mouths of the creeks, feeding on the outmigrating smolt. Later in the summer, they follow the salmon up the rivers, but they drop down again late in the season to feed on the flesh and eggs that wash down. September and October can be very productive for nice-size rainbows.

The techniques described by Chad Valentine in the next chapter work well on all the streams along the Talkeetna, as well as the many similar small creeks that flow into the Susitna, Yentna, and Skwentna.

King salmon are the prime target on most streams in the Valley. Unlike most species of salmon, kings show a wide variation in size, ranging from jacks the size of a large trout to fish that may be eight or nine years old. Susitna fish are generally not as big as the monsters that come from the Kenai. Most of them run between fifteen and thirty pounds, although a few streams, like Lake and Willow Creeks, occasionally produce fish in the fifty- to sixty-pound range. In good years, though, the fish make up in numbers what they lack in weight, with the largest runs in the Deshka River and Willow Creek.

The kings begin to run in mid-May, when the rivers are still turbid with the spring snowmelt, and the early reports whet the appetite of anglers coming out of winter hibernation. Once the rivers clear, the fishing improves dramatically, with the peak coming during late June and early July on most rivers.

The best fishing is usually found at the mouths of the rivers, where the chinook hold before moving upstream. Kings often spend days at the mouths of the rivers in which they will ultimately spawn, waiting until they are ripe before venturing into the dangers of the smaller streams. These fish become territorial and can be particularly aggressive. The mouth of a clear-water stream entering a silt-laden glacial river, which is the norm in this part of the state, will also attract fish that are still traveling upstream, giving them a chance to pump clean water through their gills.

Unfortunately, it is difficult to fish many of these areas with a fly rod. Some streams, such as Lake Creek and the Deshka, have deep water and are crowded with boats full of bait and gear fishers. On other rivers, like Willow and Sheep Creeks, the confluence with the Susitna is so overrun with anglers that it's impossible to cast a fly. Once the first flush of fish has moved upriver, though, the fly angler has a chance. There these streams transform into fast freestone rivers with good holding lies. Kings prefer the heavier water of midchannel, but resting fish still want some shelter. Look for them behind rocks, in deep pools, in the seams between currents, and along the edges of sloughs or eddies. Heavy pressure from gear and bait fishers, which is certainly to be expected on the roadside streams, often pushes kings into less desirable water. If you find a choppy riffle just upstream from heavily fished pool or run, try bouncing a fly along the bottom of the deepest section.

Cohos are second only to kings in popularity. The Susitna drainages get a run of silvers that actually exceeds the number of fish that enter the Kenai. The crowds that drifted away with the end of king season return in force for them. The best fishing is from early August through the end of the month.

Silvers congregate in fairly large schools, although not in the numbers seen with sockeyes or pinks. The most aggressive fish are those that are holding rather than migrating through, and they often show themselves by rolling on the surface. They tend to like slower water than kings or sockeyes. Look for them in the slower deep holes, near confluences with the main river, and at the outlets of feeder creeks. On larger streams, the backwater sloughs often have resting fish, usually holding in seams between currents.

On the road system, the Little Su and Montana Creek provide hot silver fishing. You'll also find silvers on Willow Creek. For more remote fisheries, try the Talachulitna River or Lake Creek. The Deshka, because of its slow-moving nature, provides lots of resting water for silvers, but don't overlook the mouth. A lot of fish hold there on their way to spawning grounds farther up the Susitna. On the Talkeetna system, Clear Creek is a good bet, but there are also fish in most of the other side streams.

Although anadromous fish are the primary targets for most anglers in the Valley, some good trout fishing is available. The roadside streams have rainbows, and a few trophies are caught every year. The implementation of no-kill regulations has helped the trout begin to return, and no place has that been more apparent than on the Talachulitna.

Trout fishing on this river had all but disappeared by the time catch-and-release was imposed, and this was the first Alaskan stream to be so regulated. Within a few years, it had been restored to one of the most productive rivers in this part of the state.

On these rivers, as on all Alaskan trout streams, the key to finding trout is to follow the salmon. Most of these rivers have only small runs of sockeyes, so the trout key on other species, particularly kings and chums. Look for the brick red color of spawning kings and drift a 10-millimeter orangish egg pattern behind them. Chums spawn in the sloughs and backwaters, and the trout will follow them in there. You won't usually see trout in these locations, which are simply too exposed, but they will be holding under any logs, cut banks, or other cover.

Because these streams get fished so heavily, the trout are usually found in the upper stretches of the rivers during salmon season. The heavy loads of glacial silt that fill the rivers during the hot summer thaw are greatly diminished during the winter. The trout that spend their summers in the clear-water streams usually winter over in the main rivers. This means that you can find some good fishing at the mouths of the creeks during the early spring, right after iceout, and again in the late fall. Early-season fish are focused on smolt and sculpins. Fall fish are looking for the eggs and flesh of dead salmon to be washed down by the autumn rains.

The Susitna drainages don't have the national reputation of other areas such as the Kenai or Bristol Bay. You won't see any articles in the national magazines about trips to these streams, but they offer some fine fishing that is easily accessible. For a visiting angler who does not wish to spend a lot of money but wants to take a salmon home, it can be a great choice.

It's not always
just about the
fish.

Sometimes it
is about the fish.
John Holman on
American Creek.

Alaskan salt water is fly fishing's undiscovered frontier.

The Karluk River, Kodiak Island. Steelhead, silvers, and bears.

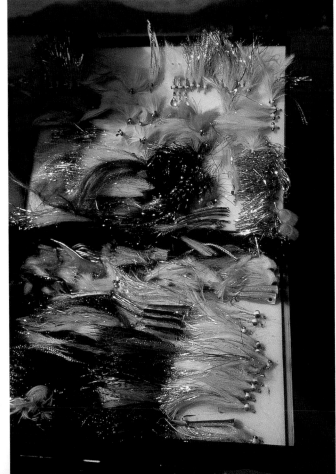

High country on the Kisaralik River. Western Alaska has the finest float trips in the state.

Saltwater fly box—no Parachute Adams or midges here.

Jack Holman's floatplanes ready for another day of chasing rainbows.

Casting fry patterns for early season rainbows.

Bears aren't the only large animals around here.

The start of another day's fishing— Bristol Bay.

Small streams, big fish. The roadside rivers of south-central Alaska have healthy runs of salmon.

Spawning sockeyes—the height of a trout fisherman's summer.

Power and beauty.

The food chain.

Dolly Varden
on a western
Alaska river.

*October on the
Kenai Peninsula.*

*A good dead
drift is the most
important
technique you
can master.*

*Releasing a
beauty.*

*Arctic char in
full spawning
regalia.*

*By fall, the trout
have grown fat on
salmon eggs.*

*Never focus so
hard on the fish
that you forget
to look around.*

*Mount St. Elias
looms over the
Lost Coast.*

A big buck coho that hit a skated dry fly.

The bodies of the salmon carry tons of nutrients from the ocean depths to the headwaters of Alaskan trout streams.

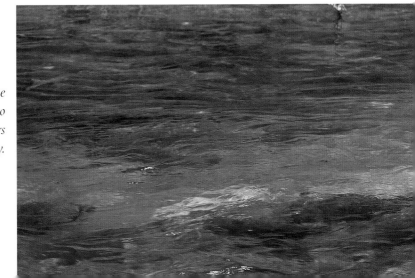

Sockeyes by the millions pour into Bristol Bay rivers in June and July.

Jeff Parker on the
Copper River.

Searching for
the perfect fly.

Trout food.

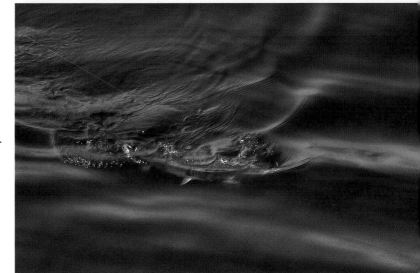

Saltwater coho.

Big rivers, big fish—a Bristol Bay rainbow.

Fall steelheading has its price.

When the salmon are running, everyone feasts.

George Davis with a happy client on Icy Bay.

Jack Holman hiking down to Moraine Creek.

Bruce Nelson getting ready for a day's float on the Kenai.

Fishing the Russian River.

11

ON THE TALKEETNA
with Chad Valentine

Talkeetna in late spring is one of those quintessential outdoor towns that are frequently featured in magazines that cater to mountain climbers, whitewater kayakers, and wilderness enthusiasts. Its streets are filled with wiry bodies and deeply tanned faces, their raccoon eyes a testament to weeks spent trying to summit North America's highest mountain. I felt a bit out of place with my fly rod and waders, but I was there to sample a lesser-known aspect of the area's outdoor charms. Situated at the confluence of the Susitna and Talkeetna Rivers, the town is the jumping-off point for exploring the drainage's numerous clear-water streams. My guide for the day, Chad Valentine, met me at his boat, tied up in an eddy bordering the throbbing current of the Talkeetna River.

Chad certainly qualifies as a local guide. He spent his first six years living in Curry, which doesn't even qualify as a wide spot in the road. It's a railroad way station, simply a bulldozed opening and a couple houses in the wilderness where the maintenance crews live. His family moved to the big city, Talkeetna, when he started school. Not counting his high school job, he has been guiding there since 1986, concentrating on the trout- and salmon-rich streams that flow into the Talkeetna and Susitna Rivers. He is part owner of Denali Angler's Lodge.

Chad and his assistant guides operate twenty-three-foot North River boats, high-speed screamers with 496-cubic-inch engines capable of fifty-five miles per hour. All that power is necessary when you're running as far as sixty miles up the Susitna and twenty-five miles up the Talkeetna, bound in only by unrunnable canyons on each river. Add in another twelve miles downstream on the Susitna, and it's a lot of water to cover. These are not slow, meandering streams, either. Both are big, glacial-flow-driven rivers, choked with snags and root balls, braiding through ever-changing gravel bars. These rivers bear no resemblance to anyone's idea of a trout stream, and the methods used to fish them are unique. It's only in the past few years that the rest of the state has discovered what Chad has known for a long time—this is some of the best trout and salmon fishing in south-central Alaska.

It was mid-May when I met up with Chad. This is not the peak time to fish these rivers, but they have the advantage of being the only running water open to trout fishing at that time of year. With one of his employees and his ever-present chocolate Lab, Rio, we ran a couple miles up the Susitna as Chad pointed out the various sloughs and feeder creeks that he fished. A lever-action 45.70, its slugs the size of a man's thumb, was tucked under the gunwale, testament to the numerous bears that wander along the river's brushy banks.

We stopped at the mouth of a small tributary, where its tannin-stained water met the gray glacial flow of the main river. Such tributaries form the backbone of the system's salmon production and the area's fishing. The little side pockets of clear water provide rearing grounds for king and silver salmon fry, as well as respite for outmigrating smolt. That means food for the river's trout and Dollies. Later in the summer, kings and silvers will hold in the same slow water. The salmon spawn in the larger tributaries, and the trout, which have wintered over in the deeper pools in the main rivers, follow them upstream.

Most of the fishing on these rivers is done at the mouths of the creeks or in the slow back channels, where the silt has had a chance to settle out and the water has cleared enough for the fish to be able to see a fly. Looking at the areas Chad pointed out as his favorite spots made it clear why it has taken so long for this fishery to develop. These are not intuitive, easily read rivers.

Spring trout fishing may be available, but it is unpredictable, completely dependent on the interplay between ice-out and runoff. The river has to be clear enough of ice for anglers to reach the creek mouths, but if the weather is too warm, the streams will blow out. The window can be short, and some years there is no fishing at all. When you hit it right, though, Chad says the fishing can be fantastic.

Our first stop yielded only a single trout, so we headed back to the confluence and then up the Talkeetna to its well-known and heavily fished tributary, Clear Creek. On this day, Clear Creek was a misnomer—the stream was running high and turbid. Chad wound the riverboat up the narrow channel, weaving between bars and snags, to the mouth of a smaller stream, optimistically called Fish Creek. This was the clean water we had been looking for. Terns were working the line between the two streams, a sure sign of outmigrating smolt. The fishing wasn't red-hot, but it was steady, and between us we managed to land some nice Dollies and lose a huge rainbow.

It was a pretty spot, and at this time of year we had it to ourselves. That sense of solitude was ephemeral, however. It would not be long before the first salmon arrived. Clear Creek is a major destination for anglers pursuing the Talkeetna's king salmon, with groups of people getting dropped off and camping along the gravel bars at the mouth. Most of the fishing is done with spinning gear and bait, and the area is so heavily used that the local bears, habituated to people, have been known to walk through camp, pick up a cooler full of food, and stroll off into the woods with it, oblivious of the crowds.

Chad knows of a number of less popular areas for kings, and many of them are fly-rod friendly. By the time the kings have gotten this far upstream, they have started to develop that brick red color that makes them easy to spot in clear water. Sight-fishing a pod of thirty kings with a fly rod at low water is an experience not to be forgotten. Those numbers are not just hype. On Chad's best day, he landed forty-two kings in five hours, all on fly rods.

Although the fish stage at the creek mouths, some of the best fishing for kings is found upstream by walking and wading to the lower pools where the fish are resting. During years with little rain, it is possible to venture well up into some truly gorgeous canyons, their tumbling waters full of migrating kings.

The kings hit the lower Talkeetna in mid-June, with the peak of the run coming about the last week of the month and the first week of July. The season closes July 13. By the time the fish get this far from tidewater, they have started to darken, although the first early-season fish can still be bright. Most of the kings average about thirty pounds, but Chad's largest was a Kenai-size seventy-two-pounder.

Fish like that require a rod with serious backbone, and Chad likes 11-weights. He uses big-game reels designed to handle tough fish in fast water. Most of the fishing is done with a sinking-tip line. The waters are not deep, but they are fast and the productive zone is usually small, so it's usually necessary to get the fly down quickly. A medium-heavy sinking-tip works well, but full-sinkers and lines like grain-weighted Teenys or Deep-Water Expresses will hang up on the rocky bottoms. It's a problem when your fly snags; it can be a disaster when your entire fly line is snagged.

Although Chad uses the typical Fat Freddies and Flash Flies rec-ommended for kings in most rivers, he also likes big leeches, tied in either Woolly Bugger or Bunny Leech style. Black and purple are his most productive colors, and he usually starts with dark flies before going to the bright stuff. His favorite is a size 1 black Woolly Bugger tied with a tungsten conehead and an orange bead behind the cone. He likes big articulated flies and has recently started to use tube flies.

The secret with kings in any river is to get the fly down to their depth. "I like to dead drift the fly on a tight line," Chad says, "letting it swing through the bottom of the run without any induced action other than the movement of the materials. If the fly stops, set the hook." The exception to dead drifting is if the fish are found milling in slack water, when a slow strip will swim the fly through the fish at mouth level.

Chad likes to look for the fish, rather than blind-fishing certain types of water. In the clear-water tributaries, this is easy to do, but even in the side channels, the fish often roll or move high enough in the water column that they can be spotted. At the mouths of the incoming creeks, the fish will lie right along the mix line between the clear incoming water and the turbid river. Low water will often keep the fish holding for a while, but a four-inch rise in the water will get them moving. This may mean that the fish holding at the mouth shoot upstream, but it may also mean that a bunch of new fish move in to replace them. It's not necessary to move around when you're fishing for kings. If you have found fish, you can usually stay with them all day. As some fish move out, new ones will move in. Unlike silvers, they do not easily spook.

Once the season for kings closes, there is a brief hiatus in activity of the primary target species. The various streams also support chums, pinks, and in a few creeks, sockeyes, but things don't heat up again until the silvers arrive about the first week in August. As with the kings, there are a few early fish, and they tend to be brighter than the fish found during the peak.

An 8-weight rod with a floating line is the rig of choice for cohos. Chad uses 12- or 14-pound tippet. The same black or purple leeches that he likes for kings work well on silvers, although they are usually tied in size 2 or 4. Fuchsia leeches, Woolly Buggers, and Bunny Flies are also good, and like every Alaskan angler, Chad carries a variety of Egg-Sucking Leeches in his fly boxes. Silvers are as fickle here as they are everywhere else, and you need to be able to switch patterns regularly.

Chad starts with a fast strip in order to trigger the aggressive nature of cohos. The fly should be allowed to sink to the level of the fish before you begin the strip. About 80 percent of the time, a fast strip is most effective, but in slow water, Chad will often dead drift a black leech through the school. There has to be just enough current to keep the fly suspended in the water column for his technique to work, but it can be very effective.

Subsurface flies are not the only way to take cohos. Skated dry flies work well, and like most fly fishers, Chad uses some variation of Pink Pollywogs most of the time. He looks for fish that are rested and lying near the surface, but he says that he's particularly looking for the occasional fish that will bite bubbles floating on the surface. Any time he sees that activity, it's a sure sign of a player, and he goes straight to a dry fly. Just twitching the fly a couple times will often induce a strike, but with silvers, variety helps. Sometimes the fish will simply come up and nose the fly, but if you get that kind of interest, keep working the fish. Hooking silvers on surface flies is not easy. Because the fish is usually coming directly toward you and you can see the strike, it's very easy to pull the fly from the fish's mouth. You need to wait for the fish to turn and get its weight on the fly before you set the hook.

Silvers prefer water that is slow moving and out of the main channel. They do not like water that is swirling, though, so any kind of fast eddy probably will not hold fish. Chad says he does a lot of sight-fishing for silvers, which seems surprising considering the heavily silted nature of the main rivers. Some of that involves spotting fish that are rolling or showing themselves in some other way, but most of it is a matter of finding clear-water sloughs and back channels and seeing the fish underwater. Many of the back channels on both the Susitna and

Talkeetna slow up enough for the water to clear, and those areas can be particularly good. It's important to be able to identify the various species, because the pools may have a mixture of cohos, chums, and pinks, and you want to be able to target your fish of choice. Unlike when fishing for kings or rainbows, Chad rarely walks up the feeder streams for silvers. There is usually very little holding water for them in the lower stretches of their spawning streams.

Silvers are much more spooky than other salmon species, particularly in shallow, calm, clear water. You need to be careful in your approach and casting. Chad says that he has seen times, however, when the whole school will go into a frenzy and fight for the fly. This erratic behavior usually lasts only about five minutes, but when it occurs, the fish will hit anything. It sort of goes with the whole mystique of silvers.

By September, the silvers are pretty much finished. Trout fishing, though, is just starting to get good. And there is surprisingly good trout fishing in these drainages. Trout fishing in Alaska is often used as a generic term for rainbows and Dollies, and the general assumption is that grayling are an enjoyable by-catch. These systems have more Dollies and grayling than rainbow, but techniques are pretty much the same for all three. There seems to be a thirty-inch ceiling on rainbows, but that's still big enough to qualify as a trophy. Dollies run up to twenty-five inches, and some grayling will get as big as twenty-one inches.

The best rainbow fishing on the Talkeetna is in the lower stretches, from Clear Creek downstream. Above that, there are fewer trout and more Dollies. The Susitna carries rainbows a bit higher, but this is right at the edge of their range. The best fishing on the Susitna is in mid- to late September, but the Talkeetna continues to improve right up to freeze-up. That's not to say there is not good midsummer fishing, though. The trout follow the kings up the streams, and if you're willing to hike up to the spawning areas, you can find some wonderful small-stream, big-fish angling.

Chad likes a 6-weight for trout and fishes them almost exclusively with a floating line. Like many guides, he prefers long rods—9 1/2 to 10 feet. They provide good casting range and help with line control. He uses a 10- or 11-foot leader. The ubiquitous pegged beads are employed behind spawning salmon. Chad puts his indicator right at the top of the leader and adds enough weight to keep the fly on the bottom. He says if you're not hanging up occasionally, you're not deep enough. Just keep varying the weight and the indicator distance until you get it right for each run you fish.

Because the fishing continues so late in the season, carcass flies see a lot of use. Chad likes Battle Creeks and white Woolly Buggers. "You should really work to get a good dead drift," he says. "Mend the line whenever necessary, then let it swing until it's hanging in the current. You will get fish all the way through the drift."

The Susitna rainbows don't have the opportunity to see a lot of sculpins, so the black leeches so common elsewhere don't get used as much here. When they do get used, however, the big patterns like sculpins and Zonkers often take larger trout than are taken on beads, albeit fewer. Some hatches occur on these streams, and late in the day, nymph fishing can be good. Occasionally you can find some dry-fly action.

Reflecting the observation of many guides, Chad says the most common mistake he sees his clients make is that "people always want to wade too deep. Ninety percent of the fish can be caught without getting your feet wet."

Chad's techniques are strikingly different from those used in many other areas, but that doesn't mean their success is limited to these two drainages. Alaska is full of glacial streams that serve as conduits for returning salmon but provide little or no fishing in the main stems. The same methods that Chad has developed for the Talkeetna will also work on the Skwentna or other rivers that are fed by clear-water streams.

For residents of Anchorage and the Mat-Su Valley, the Talkeetna and Susitna drainages offer an obvious alternative to the Kenai Peninsula streams. Wilder and more remote, the area sees far fewer anglers, and the fly-rod fishing for kings, silvers, and trout can be even more productive than on the more famous rivers to the south. If you're visiting Talkeetna and have your rod handy, check with Chad and see what's running. You might tie into some of the best fishing of your trip.

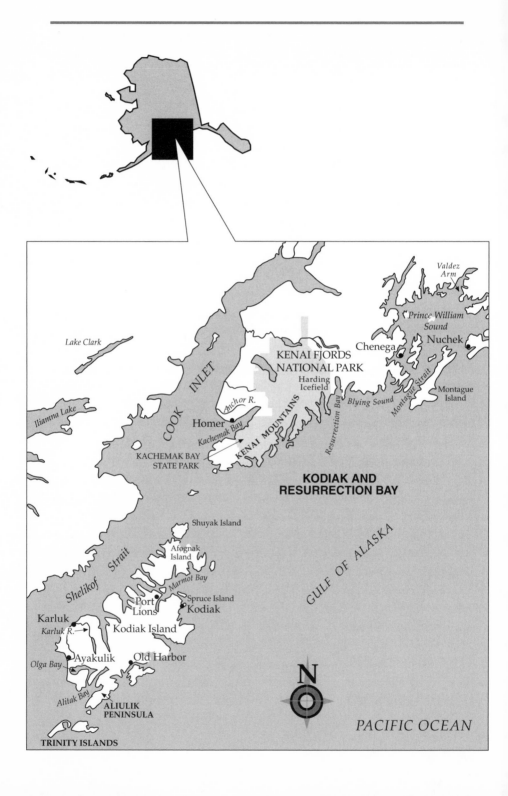

Valdez
Arm

Prince William
Sound

Lake Clark

KENAI FJORDS
NATIONAL PARK

Chenega

Nuchek

COOK INLET

Harding
Icefield

Blying Sound

Montague
Island

Iliamna Lake

Anchor R.

KENAI MOUNTAINS

Homer

Kachemak Bay

Resurrection Bay

Montague Strait

KACHEMAK BAY
STATE PARK

**KODIAK AND
RESURRECTION BAY**

Shuyak Island

Shelikof Strait

Afognak
Island

Marmot Bay

GULF OF ALASKA

Port
Lions

Spruce Island

Kodiak

Karluk

Karluk R.

Kodiak Island

Olga Bay

Ayakulik

Old Harbor

Alitak Bay

ALIULIK
PENINSULA

N

TRINITY ISLANDS

PACIFIC OCEAN

PART III

FISHING THE SALT: KODIAK AND RESURRECTION BAY

Alaska has the healthiest stocks of anadromous fish in the world—and a long tradition of fly fishing. In spite of this, very few anglers have made the transition from chasing salmon in the rivers to fishing for them in the salt. It's a curious failing. You'll find plenty of opportunities to escape the crowds on the riverbanks; salmon in salt water are not only stronger fighters, but also better eating; and the fish are feeding and will readily hit a fly.

Alaska has a lot of untapped areas, including the waters around Kodiak, in Resurrection Bay, in much of Prince William Sound, and throughout southeast Alaska. All of these areas offer the sheltered bays and straits, numerous short spawning rivers, and strong tidal currents that make this fishing possible.

Anglers take a couple different approaches to fishing the salt. Dan Busch targets fish along the shore by wading the edges near river mouths or using kickboats in the coastal lagoons. The techniques he describes will work at the outlet of any salmon stream. You'll find local variations of his methods in the interviews with George Davis and Luke Woodruff, who also spend some time fishing the outlets and estuaries along the Lost Coast and in southeast Alaska. Those same techniques will work on streams like Bird Creek and the Anchor River in south-central Alaska or along the beaches of Port Valdez.

Another approach is to use the deep-water techniques pioneered by Capt. Greg Mercer and Keith Graham. If you have a boat and some knowledge of how to locate silvers or rockfish, or you find a flexible charter captain, you can use the knowledge they have acquired to open new vistas for your own fishing. Although they fish out of Resurrection Bay, their techniques are equally applicable to Kodiak, southeast Alaska, Valdez, or Prince William Sound.

12

KODIAK ISLAND

Just a short flight south of Anchorage, between the Gulf of Alaska and the infamous Shelikof Strait, lies the Kodiak archipelago, a collection of islands that stretches almost 175 miles from north to south. Its glacier-carved mountains receive an average of seventy inches of rain a year, creating hundreds of short, clear streams that provide spawning habitat for all of Alaska's anadromous species and feeding grounds for the islands' bears.

Fishing is Kodiak's lifeblood. Surrounded by waters rich in crab, salmon, shrimp, and halibut, this is one of the greatest commercial fisheries in the world. And at least a portion of that bounty is available to the fly fisher. For the angler interested in salmon and steelhead, Kodiak is near the top of Alaska's fishing destinations, beginning with the king runs in late May and stretching through winter steelheading in November.

Three things come to mind when Kodiak is mentioned: good runs of salmon, lots of very large bears, and bad weather. There's a reason for those mental images. The salmon, particularly the pinks and cohos, arrive in numbers that will wear out the arm of any angler who arrives with them, and a couple rivers even provide excellent opportunities to take chinooks on a fly rod.

The bears are perhaps even better known. The first thing a visitor to Kodiak notices is the full-scale mount of a brown bear in the lobby of the small airport. The bear, a world record, is standing upright and about to pounce on a deer fawn. Standing next to it, you realize that you are looking up at the bear's chest. These are the largest carnivores in the world, with some of the big boars weighing over a thousand pounds. Brown bears are simply grizzlies that live close enough to the coast to survive on salmon. The abundant food source allows them to grow substantially larger than barren ground grizzlies, and nowhere do they grow larger than on these islands. They are so impressive that this race is frequently referred to simply as Kodiak bears.

Approximately three thousand bears roam the islands. Although Kodiak sees its share of bear-related tragedies, most of them are associated with hunters rather than fishers. Bears will tolerate the presence of other bears—and anglers—on a salmon stream, but they won't share a gut pile from a freshly shot deer. Needless to say, anyone planning to fish the rivers on these islands should have a good sense of bear etiquette. Bears are hunted on most parts of Kodiak, so don't expect the habituated behavior of bears from Katmai or similar parks.

The bears may be scary, but the weather can be worse. Other than those streams that cross the limited road system, access is by plane or boat. Weather delays are a regular occurrence, and when the skipper or pilot says he doesn't want to travel, you don't want to either. These guys are pros, and you should respect their judgment on safety.

Getting there is not the only weather-related problem. Its maritime climate means that Kodiak stays relatively warm but is often wet and windy. This is not a place for cheap or worn-out gear. You need to prepare for hard-driving rain, which can be an all-day, every-day occurrence, particularly during steelhead season. A raincoat that begins to leak after a couple hours isn't just an inconvenience, it's an invitation to hypothermia. Kodiak has a number of public-use cabins, and even hardcore campers recognize their comfort. That's not to say that the weather is always bad, and nothing ensures a week of sunshine like heavy-duty raingear and fleece clothes.

Fishing in Kodiak is far different from Bristol Bay or south-central Alaska. Grass-covered hills are the predominant feature. The area has some heavily wooded spruce forests—this is the northern limit of the temperate rain forest—but there is also a lot of open country. Much of the fishing is done right at tidewater, when the fish are just coming into the streams to spawn. Anglers have both roadside and remote fishing opportunities.

The largest island, Kodiak, has about one hundred miles of road system, and most of the fishing pressure occurs on the rivers accessible by car. The Pasagshak, Olds, Buskin, and American Rivers are all popular salmon fisheries, with good runs of cohos, pinks, and in some cases chums and sockeyes. The Buskin is located only a few miles south of the town of Kodiak and consequently is the most popular river on the island. It has good fishing for sockeyes, pinks, and cohos, as well as a large run of Dollies that moves into the river in late August to spawn.

The Pasagshak is a short, tidally influenced river that drains Lake Rose Tead, near the southern end of the road. It gets a run of exceptionally large silvers. Most of the fishing occurs at the mouth of the river, particularly as the fish move in on the rising tide. The lake provides a unique opportunity to fish for cohos with a float tube. The Olds River, which is closer to town, sees a lot of anglers concentrated at the mouth and along the adjoining beaches. It has good fishing for coho and Dollies in the late summer and fall. The upper river is a pretty stream flowing through a heavily forested valley and sees less pressure. American River has several miles of very fishable water. It gets so many pinks during even years that if you're looking for cohos, you may want to avoid it until the pinks have thinned out. It also has lots of small Dollies in the fall.

As in all of Alaska, the fishing improves and the crowds disappear once you leave the road system. There are several prime rivers on the main island that provide great fishing for salmon, steelhead, and Dollies. The Karluk is Kodiak's most famous river, and it comes by its reputation honestly. It has good runs of chinook and coho salmon and is perhaps the premier fall steelhead fishery in the state. Rather than flowing directly into the ocean, the Karluk enters a large tidal lagoon, and the fish mill in the stillwater before making the push upstream. This is an excellent river for a float trip, starting at either the halfway point, usually referred to as Portage, or the headwater lake.

The Ayakulik rivals the Karluk in overall productivity. It is smaller than the Karluk but has better fishing conditions along most of its length. The Ayakulik has more holding water than the Karluk, so the fish—and the fishers—tend to be spread out more than on its more famous neighbor. In addition to excellent chinook and coho fishing, it gets two runs of sockeyes, one in June and one in July. The Sturgeon

River is also a possibility. It gets the island's largest run of chum salmon and, with it, one of the largest concentrations of brown bears. Access to the Sturgeon is limited.

North of Kodiak Island is Afognak, the second-largest island in the chain. Heavily forested in places, Afognak has no settlements of any size. As with most of the other islands, narrow fjords cut deep into the heart of the mountains. Afognak has several lake-and-river systems that see good runs of sockeyes and cohos. Paul's Creek and Portage Creek are both small, clear streams with good fly-fishing potential. The runs of cohos and sockeyes are not particularly large, but the small confines of the creeks concentrate the fish and provide good sight-fishing opportunities. Both streams also see a few steelhead in the fall. The Litnik River is probably the most popular fishery on the island, with most of the fishing concentrated on the long lagoon at its mouth. The cohos mill in here before heading upstream. An ATV road provides access upstream, and fly fishing for cohos and Dollies can be good in the pools and runs of the river. There are also a number of protected and remote bays and lagoons where cohos, pinks, and sockeyes mill in the salt chuck as they stage for their final journey. Afognak has a lot of bears, and their presence is a given on every stream.

The northernmost large island is Shuyak, one of Alaska's premier recreation areas. Most of the island is designated as a state park. It has four public-use cabins, innumerable campsites, and a vendor who rents kayaks. The waters of Big Bay and Cary Inlet are protected and hold large numbers of cohos in August. Most of the fishing is in the salt, and hooking into a hot coho on a fly rod from a kayak will provide all the fight an angler could want.

The most important sport fisheries on Kodiak focus on the schools of cohos that feed in these waters, stage at the river mouths, and move upstream to spawn. These are big, tough fish, and they can be very aggressive to the fly. They can also develop an incredibly frustrating case of lockjaw, ignoring everything cast in front of them. Although anglers do a lot of deep-water fishing for cohos around Kodiak, few of the charter operators understand fly fishing. However, the techniques that Keith Graham uses so successfully in Resurrection Bay should be equally productive in waters around these islands. It's difficult to mix anglers using different techniques, but if you can fill a boat with fly rodders, there's no reason you can't pursue the fish on their feeding grounds.

As Dan Busch describes it in the next chapter, much of the best fishing is done by wading the tidal flats at low tide and intercepting the incoming fish as the water rises. In sheltered water, a small boat or even a float tube can be used to reach fish that are just beyond the reach of a long cast. In many systems, the silvers hold in lagoons that have formed near the mouth or in the narrow lakes that lie a short distance inland. These fish are tough to find but can provide some great fishing. Here again, a light boat or float tube will greatly increase the success rate.

Cohos run later on Kodiak than in many other parts of the state, and their timing varies significantly from river to river. The fishing generally starts in August, with the fish beginning to stage at the river mouths. The run peaks in mid-September, but bright fish are still showing up in many rivers well into October.

Though cohos may be the major fishery on Kodiak, it's the steelhead that draw fishers from around the world. A few spring-run fish enter the systems, but this is essentially a fall fishery. Kodiak steelhead tend to run about seven or eight pounds, although some larger fish up to fifteen pounds are taken regularly. The Karluk River is the most important steelhead destination, with up to eight thousand fish returning each fall. With a length of twenty miles from its headwater lake to the ocean, the Karluk is one of Kodiak's longest rivers. Much of it is shallow, with little in the way of the runs and slots that are required to get fast-moving steelhead to rest. The tiny pockets and cuts will often yield a fish to the exploring angler, but the bulk of the fishing is found near Portage. A couple of small cabins are available to rent near there. Much of the land around the Karluk belongs to the local Native corporation, which restricts access. Be sure to get the proper permits in advance.

Several other rivers also have steelhead, including the Ayakulik, Uganik, Dog Salmon, and Litnik Rivers. The number of returning fish range from a couple thousand on the Ayakulik to a few hundred on the Dog Salmon. In addition to these main rivers, many of the small streams that flow through spruce forest host small runs of fish. These are largely untouched fisheries, in large part because the streams each have only a few fish, which move through the fishable water so quickly that it's difficult to intercept them. Steelhead fishing peaks in October, but good fishing can be had through mid-November on some rivers.

Only two rivers have runs of chinooks. The Karluk and Ayakulik each get about twelve thousand fish returning in early summer, with the peak about mid-June. The Karluk sees more anglers, with most of the fishing concentrated in the lagoon near the mouth. The best fishing occurs near the point where the flowing water meets the incoming tide. The river can be waded here, and the kings, cohos, and sockeyes all stage right at the mouth. The lagoon also has good fishing, although it requires a boat.

The Ayakulik is probably a better bet for the fly fisher who plans to target chinooks. It gets a somewhat larger run than the Karluk, has more good holding water, is easily waded, and sees fewer anglers.

The most prolific fish in Kodiak waters is the lowly pink salmon. Disparaged by most Alaskans, pinks—or humpies, as they are often called—are actually a fun fly-rod fish if they are taken before they enter fresh water. There are few better fish for a young angler to learn on. Pinks are aggressive, scrappy, and small enough to be controlled. Many streams host runs that number in the tens of thousands, providing plenty of opportunities to keep a kid's enthusiasm up.

Pinks stage in large numbers at the mouths of practically every stream on the islands and can usually be reached from shore. The roadside streams get large numbers of fish. The run peaks in mid-August, and returns are much greater during even-numbered years. Once the pinks are on their spawning beds, they have morphed into a grotesque parody of a fish and are of little sport and no longer edible. They can be so prolific and aggressive that they prevent effectively fishing for the cohos that show up at about that time.

Dolly Varden are even more ubiquitous in Kodiak waters than pink salmon. Every stream large enough to host a few returning salmon will almost certainly hold Dollies. Although some Dollies, as well as their close cousin arctic char, are resident in Kodiak's waters, most are anadromous. Like all char, they are fall spawners, moving into the coastal streams in mid-July. Some of the best Dolly fishing occurs in late spring, as the overwintering fish ambush the fry and smolt that are migrating out to sea.

Dollies feed heavily on salmon eggs and flesh when these food sources are available. Before spawning begins, they can be taken on nymphs and occasionally dry flies, although for some reason they frequently prefer flies hanging in the current or skated on the surface. Small streamers also work well, particularly early in the year. The same techniques used for trout in other areas will work for them here. Kodiak fish are not as large as those in some other areas of the state, generally running in the fourteen- to sixteen-inch range, with some exceeding twenty inches. Dollies tend to move in schools, and a place that was hot one day may be barren the next.

Kodiak may not get much press in the fly-fishing magazines, but if you are looking for salmon or steelhead, it's difficult to think of another area that's more productive. It has road-accessible fishing and, only a short plane flight away, some of the best wilderness angling available. Add to that the tingling on the back of your neck that comes from fishing in proximity to the world's largest bears, and you have a true Alaskan experience.

13

FLY-FISHING KODIAK
with Dan Busch

Kodiak has an abundance of fish but little in the way of classic fly-fishing water. Fly fishers have had to adapt their techniques to the islands' conditions, and as a result, Kodiak has produced some of the most innovative anglers in the state. Only a handful of guides specialize in fly fishing, and Dan Busch has earned a reputation as the best of them.

Dan has lived in Kodiak since 1970. He and his wife taught high school there for years, but in 1989, he began showing guests how to take the island's prolific anadromous fish on a fly rod. Once the owner of a remote camp on Afognak, Dan now focuses on the Karluk River and the road-system streams. Attuned to the particular challenges of fishing in Kodiak, Dan uses some techniques that are not often seen in other parts of Alaska. Clients may find themselves skating dry flies for pink salmon or fishing a kickboat in the salt for cohos. If you want to catch fish on Kodiak, Dan can show you how.

I caught up with Dan at the Anchorage airport as he was returning from an extended period of sea kayaking and bonefishing in the Bahamas. He and I had both been contributors to an earlier book on Alaskan fly fishing, but this was our first opportunity to meet face-to-face. My own experience with Kodiak is limited to fishing the Karluk for steelhead, so that is where we started.

The Karluk is one of Alaska's premier steelhead rivers. Remote, and isolated by Kodiak's infamous fall flying weather, it sees relatively few anglers for the number of fish available. It flows crystal clear through rolling grassland. About two-thirds of the steelhead in the Karluk run twenty-six to twenty-nine inches, with the remainder going up to about thirty-three inches. Some larger ones are occasionally caught, though, and Dan's biggest is a thirty-seven-incher. Steelhead can be found throughout the Karluk, but there's not a lot of holding water at the lower end and in the canyon. The best water is near Portage, but that's private land, and you need to purchase a permit from the local Native corporation in order to fish there.

Although the Karluk is the premier steelhead stream on Kodiak, almost every system with a lake has some fish. The Ayakulik is the second most productive river, although it is somewhat featureless. Most of the fishing is around Bear Creek. Other streams with sizable runs include the Litnik and Afognak Rivers, but they too have little holding water, so the fish tend to move through quickly.

The steelhead begin returning to the Karluk in September. Fish and Game operates a weir in the lower river to count salmon returns, but once it is removed early in the month, the fish are free to move upstream. The steelhead are accompanied by a burst of silver salmon, so September fishing is a mixed bag, with both silvers and steelhead competing for your flies. The steelhead stay in the river over the winter and spawn in the spring, which means more fish in the late than earlier in the year. By the third or fourth week in October, the fishing is at its peak. Most of the silvers are gone by then, so anglers concentrate on the sea-run rainbows.

Depending on water conditions and client preference, Dan uses one of three techniques for steelhead. The first is the traditional sinking-tip and wet-fly swing. This is the easiest method of fishing, in large part because the tight line makes it easier to detect the often subtle strikes.

He likes large, flowing flies with lots of inherent action—Egg-Sucking Leeches, Articulated Leeches. Some of these flies may be four to five inches long and are usually weighted with a conehead or lead eyes. Both bright and dark colors are effective, and Dan carries flies primarily in hot pink, fuchsia, cerise, black, and purple. "I usually start with a large bright fly, and if that doesn't draw strikes, I will go to a dark fly," he says. "If neither of those is of interest to the fish, I will drop down to smaller flies in the same colors."

The Karluk is not a deep river, and a heavy sinking-tip is not necessary. Dan likes a variation of the classic across-and-down wet-fly swing, though. By casting at forty-five degrees upstream, his fly is on the bottom and in the fish's zone as the line comes directly across the current, giving the fish a broadside view of the fly. At the end of the swing, he lets the fly hang, but in another variation of traditional technique, he strips the fly three or four times and then lets it drop back. Dan also fishes egg patterns with a sinking tip, usually something that imitates a cluster of eggs, which may be nothing more sophisticated than a gob of yarn tied to the hook.

The second method that Dan uses is a floating line with a strike indicator and a Glo-Bug or bead. This is dead drift fishing that is particularly effective where there is a distinct seam or holding lie that can be explored thoroughly. Egg patterns are the same size as the naturals or slightly larger, but in addition to the usual colors used for trout, Dan likes to give the steelhead something different. Surprisingly, he says blue can be a very good color. Some of his Glo-Bugs are tied with two colors to create a sense of depth in the fly. Just as with traditional wet flies, Dan changes colors when he is not getting strikes.

Dan also fishes beads as egg patterns, but he acknowledges that they are controversial with many fly fishers. He is careful never to peg the bead more than an inch above the hook, and he says that fish are invariably hooked in the side of the mouth. It's only when several inches are left between the bead and the hook that there are problems with fish being hooked in the eyes or gills. He finds that beads are less damaging to fish than some of the big leeches, which fish can take deep.

Even with a strike indicator, it's not easy to detect the strikes of steelhead. One additional problem is the difficulty in setting the hook, particularly on a downstream cast. The fish usually just mouth the egg pattern, and the strike has a tendency to pull the hook up and out of the fish's mouth.

The final technique that is useful on the Karluk is also the least used. If the water is relatively warm, in the forties, you can get a fish to rise to a skated dry fly—an unusual opportunity with Alaskan steelhead. It requires finding fish in fairly shallow water, no more than a foot and a half to two feet deep, with a slick surface and a moderate current. Most of the common steelhead drys, such as Bombers, will work. Dan likes to use a Muddler tied with a riffle hitch. The fish target the motion and not the color, but Dan uses dark flies rather than the hot pink skaters that are so effective on cohos. The flies can be fished by simply not mending the line and just allowing the drag to skate them, or they can be stripped across slower water. It takes some patience to keep fishing a dry, particularly when other anglers are hooking up by using traditional techniques, but the reward of a big steelhead boiling on a surface fly is well worth it.

Regardless of the technique he is employing, Dan is a strong advocate of a long rod. He uses an 11 ½-foot, single-handed, 8/9-weight for steelhead and cohos. It gives him great line speed for casting into the ever-present Kodiak wind, and it allows him to mend the line easily and effectively. He also ties his own leaders. For fishing with a floating line and strike indicator, he uses at least a 12-foot leader, tied with sections of 20-, 16-, and 12-pound hard Mason with a tippet of 8- or 10-pound Maxima. Tippets are tied on with a loop-to-loop. Sinking-tip leaders are much shorter and tied with little or no taper, but they also have a butt section of the stiffer Mason and a tippet of the more flexible Maxima. In both cases, the stiff butt and taper help the fly turn over, and the softer tippet allows more movement in the water.

One recurring theme in Dan's discussion of this type of fishing echoes famed steelheader Lani Waller's advice about the necessity of fishing with confidence. "Having confidence is so important—much more so than anglers realize. Using a fly or technique you have confidence in means that you are attuned to what's happening. You know how the fly is drifting, and it's easy to make the adjustments necessary to get the fly right in front of the fish. Whether you are using a sinking-tip, indicator, or dry fly, a lack of confidence expresses itself in lackadaisical, sloppy fishing, and the steelhead gods hate it when that happens."

Steelhead are the Holy Grail of Kodiak fly fishing, but silver salmon are far more common. They are available in all of the larger rivers and pretty much every stream that has a lake somewhere in the system. The timing of the runs varies dramatically, with fish showing up offshore at Afognak and Shuyak in late July and early August. By contrast, the fish don't arrive at the mouth of the Karluk until September, a four- to five-week time differential. Most of the streams on Kodiak Island are late, but there is some variation from river to river.

Although many anglers pursue cohos in the road-system rivers, Dan focuses on the fish that are still staging in the salt water or are holding in flat stillwater like the Pasagshak Lagoon. Rivers like the Buskin and Olds get good runs, but they are freestone streams and don't have a lot of the pools and back eddies that hold fish. Silvers, unlike sockeyes, are best fished in slow water, and given Kodiak's steep terrain, that means salt water, the lagoons, or lakes. Larger rivers, like the Karluk, do hold fish and can be fished in a traditional manner.

Most of Dan's coho fishing, particularly in the early season, is done by wading the salt water. He likes to walk the shoreline in the bays and coves near the mouth of a spawning stream, looking for fish that are showing, betraying their presence by jumping and rolling. The trick is to intercept the moving school. If the streams are low, silvers will often congregate and hold in the bays, sometimes for a couple weeks, waiting for a good rain to raise the rivers.

In protected waters, a kickboat is a great way to get to those fish that are holding a hundred yards offshore. Many people fish float tubes by casting back into the water that they've just floated over. That may work for trout, but the silvers will be long gone. It's important to get your fly to fish that are not aware of your presence, so long casts are an asset. Landing a fish with the strength of a fresh silver from a float tube is always an adventure, and Dan says that a few rods get broken every year. Carry a spare in the car. These are cold waters that will suck the heat from your body. If you plan to spend the day bobbing in a float tube, you'll need plenty of insulation. Dan has gone to thick pile pants and Gore-Tex waders, but he says there's still a place for neoprene near the end of the season.

Unlike fish that have entered fresh water, the silvers holding in the bays are still feeding. The best flies are those that imitate the herring, sand lances, and other baitfish on which the silvers are feeding. Clousers, Deceivers, and epoxy-headed flies like the ALF series are effective. Dan points out a critical part of fishing for feeding cohos: "Silvers often take the fly on the drop, so the best retrieve is strip, strip, and then let the fly drop. You need to keep your line tight, though, to feel the strike."

Fishing for silvers has changed dramatically since the discovery of their willingness to hit surface patterns. Fortunately, they are just as aggressive toward Pink Pollywogs in salt water as they are in fresh. Dan estimates that he can fish the surface about 25 percent of the time. Dry-fly fishing requires undisturbed fish. Look for rested fish lying on the surface; you'll sometimes see their dorsal fins sticking out of the water. Once the fish are stirred up and excited, their willingness to hit any kind of fly, dry or wet, drops dramatically. The best surface patterns are a variation on Henry Ford's famous saying: Cohos will hit any color as long as it's pink. Pink Pollywogs and pink poppers with marabou tails are Dan's favorites. He uses a 12-foot leader with 10-pound Maxima as the tippet.

As the fish start to move into the rivers, Dan focuses on the tidal areas, where he can catch them just coming in on the tide. Although most of the rivers have rocky bases, some have silt-laden, mucky bottoms that can be tricky wading. Tidal-area lagoons are also productive. Some lakes, such as Lake Rose Tead on the Pasagshak, provide excellent fishing, particularly from a float tube or kickboat.

Once the fish move into fresh water, they stop feeding, and the baitfish patterns that were so alluring in the ocean don't draw much attention. Silvers are notoriously fickle, so Dan, like most guides, uses a variety of flies. He starts with leeches, including the same articulated patterns that are so effective for steelhead. He says that almost any color works at some time, but he likes the hot pinks, cerise, and green for bright flies and black and purple as dark variations. If the fish aren't hitting the larger flies, he drops down to sparse nymphlike flies tied as small as size 8. Use a heavy wire hook, or those big cohos will straighten it out.

Just as you have to keep changing flies with silvers, you also need to change your retrieve. Dan starts with a slow strip, and then speeds it up and varies the rhythm until he finds something that the fish want at that particular time. With the very small flies and stillwater, he likes a slow retrieve. Silvers can occasionally be leader-shy, and with a size 6 or 8 pattern, he may go as light as 6-pound tippet.

Silvers are much more attuned to their surroundings than some other species and are easily disturbed. A fish that sees you is unlikely to hit, so it's important to stay low and cast long. The splash of a poorly cast fly will turn silvers off, particularly when they are resting on the surface. Silvers in the salt are somewhat less sensitive, because they are constantly moving, but they still need to be approached with care. Overworked fish will also go off the bite and need to be rested. If they won't hit, it's better to go look for fresh fish and let your targets settle down. Dan goes so far as to say that they share some of the frustrating characteristics of New Zealand trout—which are notoriously spooky.

One of Dan's favorite quarries is pink salmon, which he calls "the most overlooked sport fish in Alaska." Pinks run in even-numbered years and are ubiquitous in Kodiak streams. He fishes them exclusively in the salt. Pinks spawn in the intertidal areas, so they begin to deteriorate as both a food and sport fish as soon as they taste fresh water. In the ocean, though, they will provide hours of fun on a 5-weight. Because they occur in such large numbers and are easy to fool, they are great fish for kids and beginners. You can count on instant rewards when you find a school of pinks.

Dan looks for fish at the mouths of the systems in which they spawn. Pinks stage in the bays before running upstream, and because they show and jump frequently, they are easy to spot. Incoming tides will often bring them in close to the stream mouth.

It is Dan's twist on catching pinks that changes them from a kid's fish into a serious fly-rod target. He uses dry flies. Dan says that pinks that are rolling or showing on the surface will eagerly attack a skated dry. He prefers a fly resembling a large pink caddis, but simple skaters tied out of a strip of pink foam and some marabou also work well. He fishes these flies with a floating line and 6-pound tippet.

If drys don't work, Dan goes to a wet fly, still on the floating line. Exact imitations are not required for pinks, and Dan likes a simple fly tied with bead-chain eyes and red Sparkle Yarn extended as a tail. A pearlescent Flashabou overbody gives the fly some flash. If you want a more realistic pattern, a Pink Shrimp tied with black bead-chain eyes at the back of the hook works well. A couple strands of a stiff material for antennae complete the fly.

Whether you skate dry flies for pink salmon or swing a Bunny Leech for steelhead, Kodiak has some of the best accessible fishing for anadromous fish in the state. The techniques needed there may be a bit different, but with the benefit of Dan's years of experience and experimentation, a visiting angler can take advantage of its great opportunities.

14

SALT WATER:
Fly Rods and Deep Water

Salt water is the last great unexplored frontier of Alaskan fly fishing. That's a bit surprising, given that the thousands of miles of coastline provide some of the most rewarding fisheries in the state. The fish can be plentiful and eager, and the scenery is invariably spectacular. In some areas, such as Valdez and Resurrection Bay, freshwater fishing for the prime species—usually silver salmon—is prohibited, so the only opportunity for quality fly fishing is in the salt, either along the beaches or out in open water. Most people consider a fly rod to be a handicap in the ocean, but the truth is that in the right spot, a good fly fisher will often catch more than the trollers and party-boat bait drowners.

The most common form of saltwater fly fishing is along the shoreline, usually right at the mouth of a stream, targeting fish that are returning to spawn. Most of the fishing along the beaches is done by wading, but in protected waters, a kickboat or even a kayak will allow you to get to fish that are holding a bit off the beach. Small skiffs are common in much of Alaska and provide a more stable casting platform than a sea kayak. Look for fish in the estuaries and along the beaches, particularly where a point or rocky outcropping will concentrate fish. A sheltered bay has the potential for some good saltwater fishing, at least if a spawning river empties into it.

The beaches and river outlets are not the only saltwater fishing available. There is also great fishing among the straits, channels, bays, and islands that make up areas like southeast Alaska, the Kodiak archipelago, Resurrection Bay and Kenai Fjords, Prince William Sound, and Valdez Arm. Pink and silver salmon are the principal targets, but you can also find rockfish, halibut, and lingcod. The fishing may be great, but almost none of it is done with a fly rod. In spite of the worldwide explosion of saltwater fly fishing in the past decade, it is only beginning to be explored in Alaska. That's unfortunate, because under the right conditions, it can be one of the most enjoyable fly-fishing experiences available.

This is near-shore fishing, with the boat rarely more than half a mile from land. But the steep-to slopes of many areas mean that you are in deep water. The rich marine ecosystems provide an added bonus, with abundant wildlife on display. Humpback whales, orcas, and sea lions are found throughout these waters. Murres, puffins, kittiwakes, and other seabirds compete with the salmon for food. Combine this with the stunning vistas of spruce-covered mountains, blue water, and glaciers, and you have one of the most rewarding fishing opportunities in Alaska.

Cohos are the first choice for a fly rodder. They are more common and more predictable than kings, so it's easier to find them. Cohos tend to hunt near the surface, in the upper forty feet of the water column. They are aggressive feeders and will readily hit a baitfish pattern. A hooked fish will often bring its schoolmates within range of other anglers on the boat. When the cohos are around, the fishing can be hot and heavy.

Cohos are widespread, but finding them in a big ocean is not easy. If the fish are very close to the surface, you may see them rolling or jumping. More commonly, the birds will give away their presence. Puffins, kittiwakes, and murres feed on the bait pushed upward by the salmon. Circling gulls are a sure sign, but even birds sitting on the water can indicate fish. Puffins and murres dive from the surface rather than from the air, so watch for them to disappear and pop back up.

Rocky coastlines are the best places to look, and fishers around Kodiak, Resurrection Bay, and most of southeast Alaska have plenty of options. The points and capes force feeding fish into a narrow path, and any underwater structure that concentrates the bait will usually draw the migrating salmon. The same factors apply to the straits between islands. The tide rips that form along the back sides of rocks and islands can be particularly good. The fish will hold right along the seam between the two currents. Kelp beds hold lots of small fish, and silvers can often be found hunting along their edges. Bays and estuaries, particularly those with a spawning stream, are also obvious places to look.

Fish finders, depth sounders, and GPS units are the keys to consistently getting onto the fish. They allow you to identify likely spots and return to them on future trips. Success depends on finding some type of structure or current that concentrates the fish, usually because it concentrates the bait on which they are feeding. Cohos tend to follow the same migration patterns from their offshore feeding areas back to their natal streams, appearing in the near-shore area weeks before they move into fresh water. Bottom configurations and tidal currents don't vary from year to year, and the same conditions that attracted the schools of baitfish one year will fish well the next. Keep notes on the tidal currents as well as the coordinates of your hot spots.

Pink salmon are rarely targeted in deep water, but they are commonly found in the same places as cohos. Kings can also be taken on a fly rod, but they tend to stay deeper than the silvers and are much harder to locate. The best shot at them is near the mouths of the spawning rivers. The fish stage there and can often be found at a depth shallow enough to fish with a fly rod.

Rockfish provide some of the best and most predictable saltwater fly fishing. There are dozens of species in Alaska, but the most common fly-rod quarry is black rockfish, also called black sea bass. They are very common, though they are vulnerable to overfishing. Rockfish are generally a deep-water fish, but they can be found at depths of thirty to forty feet. They can often congregate in schools so large that you need only get a fly to the proper depth to hook up. Good rockfish will run seven or eight pounds and put a pretty good bend in your rod. The added bonus is that they are great eating.

Finding rockfish is much easier than locating salmon. The pinnacles and rockpiles that show up on the depth sounder or NOAA charts are the places to start. The best are those that rise up out of deep water to a depth of thirty feet or so. Rockfish will congregate at the tops of these pinnacles, usually on the downstream side. Kelp beds are also good places to look.

Frequently the only difference between catching cohos and rockfish is the amount of time you let the fly sink. An extra few seconds will put your fly below the salmon and into the rockfish. This is not a hard-and-fast rule, however. Rockfish will chase bait or chum to the surface, making it easier on you and the fish. Bringing deep-water fish like rocks to the surface quickly can burst their air bladders, making it impossible to safely release them. Some skippers will chum up the fish first so that they become adapted to surface pressures, and the smaller fish can be safely turned loose.

Occasionally a hooked fish that you have been bringing up easily will suddenly make a powerful surge for the bottom. Meet the competition. Big lingcod lie in the rocks below the schools of sea bass, and any fish struggling at the end of a line is fair game. Needless to say, anything that thinks of five-pound fish as bait is more than you can handle on an 8-weight. If you want to target lings, bring a 10- or 12-weight.

Very little special tackle is required for this type of fishing. An 8- or 9-weight rod will work as well in the salt as it does for silvers in the rivers. These fish don't normally make the screaming runs of a bonefish, so any reel with a good-quality drag will work. The only equipment a freshwater fisher needs to add to the tackle box is a 350- or 450-grain sinking line and some baitfish patterns tied on saltwater hooks. The deep-water techniques described by Keith Graham and Greg Mercer in the next chapter will work pretty much anywhere you can find fish.

Because there has been so little exploration of the fly-fishing possibilities, very few charter operators have any expertise. They do know how to find fish, however, which is far more critical. Just make sure that the skipper knows of some hot spots where the fish are within thirty or forty feet of the surface. You also need a boat with a minimum of obstructions that might interfere with your casting. Even roll casting requires overhead room. Once you find a skipper who is interested, the next project is to find enough friends to fill the boat. It's possible to synchronize fly casting so that several people can fish simultaneously, but it's almost impossible to mix fly fishing with other types of offshore tackle.

Salt water is the last frontier of Alaskan fly fishing, and it is one well worth exploring. It's the best, if not the only, game in town in some areas—but its appeal goes well beyond that. Even hard-core stream fishers like me find it an exciting and productive alternative. The fish are tough, and the action can be nonstop. Even if you have a slow day, it gives you an opportunity to see some of the most spectacular scenery in the state. And if you get a chance to fish with people like the ones in this book, it's an added bonus.

15

FISHING THE NEAR SHORE
with Keith Graham and Capt. Greg Mercer

Coffee in hand, my fishing buddy Bob and I joined the early-morning crowd in the Seward small-boat harbor. A thick coat of fog enshrouded the boats, leaving the breakwater a ghostly shadow. It was the first day of the Seward Silver Salmon Derby, and the docks were crowded with hopeful anglers. I didn't see any other fly rods, but that wasn't surprising. This is traditionally a bait and gear fishery.

We joined Keith Graham, the owner of Worldwide Angler in Anchorage, and Cindi Squire, an avid fly fisher, aboard the Quarterdeck, a twenty-six-foot Grady White powered by twin 130-horse Hondas. One of our party was unable to make it, so Keith got an opportunity to fish. Capt. Greg Mercer welcomed us aboard and seemed as excited as the rest of us. Keith and Greg have teamed up to provide one of the few opportunities available to chase silvers and rockfish with a fly rod. I had seen photos from previous trips, and it was clear that this was an adventure worth trying.

As we headed out in the soup, the radar showed a fleet of tiny boats scattering as they left the harbor. By the time we reached the end of Resurrection Bay, an hour's run away, the fog had lifted enough to see the spruce-covered granite of the shoreline mountains. The land goes straight up from the bay here, and we knew it went straight down as well. It's a near-shore fishery, but it has blue-water depth. Finding fish would be determined by locating the undersea pinnacles, rocky points, or current rips that concentrated prey and brought predators into range.

Our boat slid past groups of small islands, a few trees and shrubs clinging to their sheer, rocky sides. Gulls wheeled overhead, guillemots beat past us, and puffins pattered their way across the water, trying to avoid us. In one cove, a pod of sea lions splashed lazily. We kept a sharp eye out for the humpback whales that are common in the area, but none appeared.

We had entered Kenai Fjords National Park, one of Alaska's most scenic—but little seen—areas. At the heads of most of the long, narrow bays, massive glaciers slowly ease their way down to the waterline, calving icebergs that began their journey high in the Harding Icefield.

The weather can be tough in these waters, even in summer, but we had lucked out. Greg said that once every couple weeks, the wind blows hard enough that he is restricted to fishing in the bay. Fortunately, as the weather worsens in late August, the bay becomes more productive and can offer great fishing.

Forty minutes later, after passing several groups of boats working coves and points, we came to half a dozen boats congregated together in a channel between groups of islands. People lined the rail on each of the boats, mooching with cut bait. "I found this spot several years ago and had it to myself for a couple seasons," Greg told us. "Then some guy I hired and gave the GPS coordinates to got drunk in the bar with his buddies, and now look at it. We can work around them, though."

We grabbed our rods from the holders as Greg maneuvered the boat into a likely drift. Keith had provided us with 8-weight rods equipped with Teeny saltwater 450-grain sinking lines. We started with the weighted chartreuse and white Clousers he had rigged. Four people casting from a twenty-six-foot boat requires coordination, and at its best, it is not an elegant proposition. We managed somehow to get our lines in the water and began throwing stack mends to allow them to sink to depth. The currents carried our lines from the boat as they sank, and when they had reached depth, we began to retrieve.

"Strip it back as fast as you can," Keith instructed us. "Sometimes it even helps to hold the rod under your arm and strip in with both hands." It was only the second or third cast before Cindi let out a happy yelp. "Nice silver," she said.

Bob and I were not far behind. The fish hit hard, smashing the fleeing flies. These were big, strong fish, most about ten or twelve pounds, although silvers in the eighteen-pound range are caught every year during the derby. As our fish came to the boat, their schoolmates followed. We could see them flashing under the boat, chasing bait about ten feet down. Doubles were not unusual, and on one occasion all four of us had fish on at the same time. Glancing up at the other boats, we realized that there were not a lot of bent rods. Between our observations and the chatter on the radio, it soon became obvious that we were catching far more fish than any of the people using live bait.

Silvers weren't the only fish of the day. If we let the line sink deeper, we started catching rock bass. These were heavy-bodied, dusky rocks that put a serious bend in an 8-weight rod. They are great eating fish, but they grow slowly and are susceptible to overharvest. Rockfish are so willing to hit a fly or bait that it's possible to fish them out of a particular rockpile, so Greg took only a few fish from each spot. On a couple occasions, a smaller rockfish was being brought up when it suddenly dove for the bottom—in all likelihood the victim of a large lingcod. It is Jurassic Park down there among the boulders.

When Keith and Greg started running fly-rod trips three years ago, they billed them as rockfish trips, with silvers considered a bonus. Keith says, though, that they have hit salmon on every trip to date and have even taken the occasional king salmon. The sport is so untapped that they are currently running only four fly-rod trips a season. We got a lot of interest from the other skippers on the dock at the end of the day. Several of them said that they use fly tackle when they take out their families on their days off.

When we got a break in the action, I asked Keith and Greg about the tackle and techniques they recommend. Keith says he prefers 8-weight rods, although he carries a couple 10-weights aboard for lingcod. Getting the fly down to the right depth is the secret for both salmon and rockfish. The heavy Teeny lines combined with weighted flies are essential for success. Keith likes to use 17-pound-test level leaders, usually about 5 to 7 feet long. He has occasionally gone to fluorocarbon when the fish are particularly difficult, but generally they are not leader-shy.

Flies are tied on 2/0 and 3/0 hooks, and unlike freshwater salmon flies, they are designed to closely imitate the baitfish. Herring and sand lance are the usual prey. The most productive flies are Articulated Hareball Leeches, Clousers in white and in chartreuse and white, and Flashtail Minnows. Keith's fly box also included Crease Flies and various epoxy-headed saltwater patterns, such as Sea Habit Bucktails and ALFs.

Rockfish aren't too picky, and the same patterns that work for silvers will fool them. It's often necessary to anchor over a likely spot, however, and when the currents are running, even a 450-grain sinking-tip won't get down. Tie a few patterns with very heavy heads—essentially jigs. You may not be able to cast them, but they will dive deep enough to get into the fish.

Keith had us cast the 30-foot sinking head upcurrent and then stack mend as the tip sank. The drift of the boat pulled the line out, so that by the time we reached the backing, we were at an appropriate depth and could make a reasonably long retrieve. Retrieves were as fast as we could strip in the line. "A scared baitfish is going full out," Keith says. "So if you slow down the retrieve, it looks unnatural and gives the salmon a chance to look at the fly. They will almost always refuse to hit a fly that stops. At times, though, they will follow a fly that's diving, and when you start the retrieve, they will hit it as soon as it moves. It probably looks like a stunned baitfish that's about to escape."

Silvers are aggressive fish, and they will hammer a fleeing fly. By stripping the flies fast, we ensured that the biggest and fastest fish—which meant adult silvers—were able to get to our flies first. The moochers in the party boats were catching a lot of smaller pink salmon—and having their bait stolen by them. By contrast, we hooked only one pink all day. Our flies were almost always chased by immature salmon, about twelve inches long. Schools of them would swirl under the boat whenever a fly was retrieved. Although they would nip the tails of the flies, we rarely hooked them, but the added flash and excitement seemed to stir up the adult fish.

Like silvers in fresh water, the ocean fish are very light-sensitive. During the early-morning fog, the fish were at a shallow depth, and we frequently caught sight of schools flashing by underneath us. On several occasions, we watched the big silvers slam our flies just as they reached the boat. By about 11:00, though, the sun began to burn through, lighting up the hillsides. As the day turned into a rare combination of calm and bright sunshine, the fish went deep, dropping from about ten feet to the twenty- to twenty-five-foot depth that is more typical of silvers. We let the flies go down to reach them and began picking up more rockfish.

It was soon obvious that a big part of our success was Greg's knowledge of the water. Boats a few hundred yards away were doing nothing while we were on our way to limiting out. I asked him what he looks for in discovering new places to fish.

"Structure and currents are the keys," he says. "Most of the places we've been fishing have underwater pinnacles that attract the bait. A lot of them are charted, but hundreds are still unmarked. I keep an eye on the depth sounder, and when I see a new one, I mark it on the GPS. If I find a likely one and the tide is right, I will drift the pinnacle to see if we pick up fish. There's a lot of trial and error, but over the years, I've found a number of good spots."

It was obviously true. We had run for an hour and a half to get to the first spot, but over the course of the day, we didn't move more than a mile or so for the various drifts. Greg focused on water near a point of land that marked the entrance to one of the larger bays. That point funneled fish into a narrow area, concentrating them over the structure we were fishing.

"Currents are critical, and with the big tides we get in Alaska, the water can move pretty fast. I like to fish the back sides of the pinnacles when the tide is running. The baitfish get tumbled around as they wash over the rocks, and the big predators just lie there and scoop them up. If the current is too strong to get a good drift, I'll anchor up to stay over the right spot. Sometimes the hot zone is no bigger than a tennis court."

Greg also says that birds are a good indicator of baitfish locations. "They don't have to be flying; just birds on the water will often mark good fishing." That was borne out by the dozens of puffins and flocks of gulls and murres that surrounded us whenever we were on fish. We would watch the puffins tip up and dive on the bait, frequently reappearing with small fish trapped crosswise in their stubby bills. At times the birds show Greg big bait balls, and he parks the boat in the middle of the frenzy. "When that happens, you get salmon working the bait, rock bass coming up from deeper water for them, and big lingcod coming up for the rock bass. Things can get pretty wild."

Catch-and-release of salmon is not allowed in salt water, and by midday we had our limit of silvers. Greg anchored up over one of his favorite rockfish spots. The fish finder showed a huge school of bass below the boat. Bringing fish up from deep water quickly causes their swim bladders to expand rapidly and can be very hard on them. Greg chopped up some frozen herring and pitched the chum overboard, hoping to bring the fish closer to the surface before we started fishing. Because they come up more slowly, they can adapt to the gradual decrease in pressure. Catching them at shallower depths allows the smaller fish to be released unharmed. Even so, the fast currents meant that we needed heavily weighted flies to get down.

The heavy, hard-fighting rock bass were the perfect way to end the day. On the way back in, I asked Greg about the opportunities to fly-fish in salt water. He says that very few skippers have any experience, but he expects to see more and more boats offering fly-fishing trips as the demand increases. In the meantime, he has some suggestions for those who would like to put a trip together. "Four people is about the maximum number that can fish without getting hopelessly tangled. And even then, you need people with some experience. If I have inexperienced casters on board, I will often just anchor up over a pinnacle and let the current take the lines out. A simple roll cast is all you need in that case. If we're on rockfish, I will usually try to chum the fish closer to the surface. With better casters, I prefer to drift with the current so the fly has a more natural motion to it."

Greg offers some advice on the best kind of boat for such fishing. "Look for a boat that's no more than twenty-eight or thirty feet long. A boat larger than that requires more people to pay the freight. Unless you're fishing in some sheltered spot close to home, you want a boat that's at least twenty-four feet or so for safety reasons. Even in the summer, we can get some bad weather in Alaska. A full walk-around is important, because these silvers can run you completely around the boat."

He also notes what to look for in a skipper. "A captain with fly-fishing expertise is obviously preferable, because he knows the strengths and limitations of using flies. But if no one like that is available, I would look for a skipper that has extensive experience with conventional gear. He is more likely to have a batch of uncharted pinnacles logged into his GPS. With a fly rod, you're limited to fairly shallow depths, and the more well-known bits of structure have usually been beat up by the party boats. I add ten or fifteen new locations to my list each summer so I have places that are relatively shallow and haven't been fished."

Greg recommends booking early. "Most of the skippers with smaller boats fill up with halibut or salmon charters during the winter, so you may have trouble with last-minute arrangements. Saltwater fly-fishing trips are great for visitors who have spent a few days fishing the rivers and want to try something different."

By the time we got back to Seward, the day breeze had picked up and the sailboats were out. The dock was a mass of anglers watching as the crews filleted out salmon, bass, and lingcod, but there was not another fly rod in sight. They don't know what they're missing.

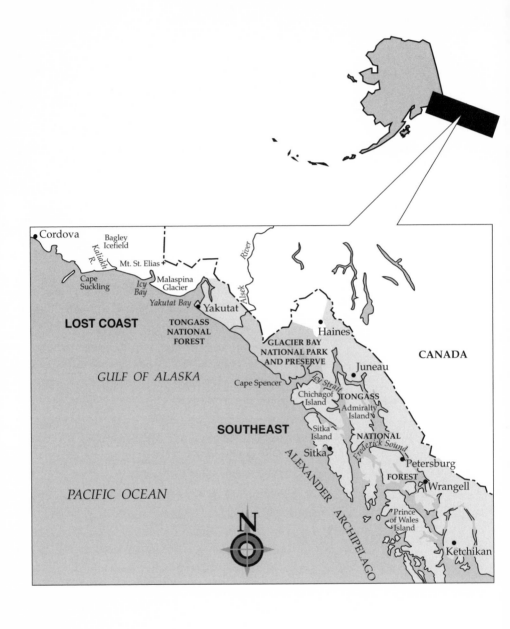

PART IV

SOUTHEAST ALASKA AND THE LOST COAST

The waters that stretch from Cordova, at the western edge of the Gulf of Alaska, to Ketchikan, at the southern tip of Alaska's panhandle, have a lot of untapped fly fishing. Most of the fishing in these parts of the state occurs within a mile or so of tideline. With the exception of the Situk River near Yakutat, there are no true destination streams for fly fishers, but good—and in some cases, spectacular—fishing can be had.

Between Cordova and Yakutat, the coast is a long line of wave-pounded beaches. Few people venture into this country, but the fishing for big cohos is unrivaled. Travel here invariably means beach landings in small planes and bouncing rides in all-terrain vehicles. An adventurous spirit is a prerequisite to fishing the Lost Coast. George Davis, one of Alaska's most innovative guides, has fished it his entire life. He explains the secrets of skating dry flies for trophy-size silvers.

Southeast Alaska is a far different landscape—a maze of wilderness islands with thousands of short, productive streams; a few larger rivers; and an intricate coastline. Although the Alaskan ferries, cruise ships, fishing boats, and pleasure craft all ply the waters of the Inside Passage, it's rare to see more than another boat or two in any cove or bay. You'll find cutthroat trout and Dolly Varden in place of rainbows, and silver salmon and steelhead range throughout the region. Most visitors arrive on massive cruise ships that dock at the various towns, but the area's beauty also draws kayakers, campers, and sailors. Luke Woodruff knows the tiny creeks around Juneau, and his techniques will work on any of the steep rain-forest streams found throughout southeast Alaska or in places like Kodiak or Prince William Sound.

16

YAKUTAT
AND THE LOST COAST

The Lost Coast comes by its name honestly. Lacking the protective islands of southeast Alaska, it is fully exposed to the often-frightening waters of the Gulf of Alaska. Piles of huge driftwood logs tossed high on the beach are evidence of the power of the winter storms. Even the geographic names are intimidating: Icy Bay, Dangerous River, Disenchantment Bay. Behind the beaches and bays are the ice-covered peaks of the Fairweather Range and Wrangell–St. Elias. There may be no more rugged and beautiful place to fish in Alaska.

The fish match the country. No insect-sipping rainbows here. These waters are home to big, brawling anadromous fish, primarily cohos and steelhead. Just inside the pounding surf, where the fish are still bright chrome and covered with sea lice, a fly rodder can easily become worn out. For those fishing the famed Situk, deep, snag-protected holes provide havens for Alaska's largest run of steelhead. Farther up the coast, in Icy Bay and along the Tsiu River, large skated dry flies are the choice for silver salmon.

Yakutat has long been a well-known destination for anglers. Alaska's largest run of steelhead enters the river in May and June, and from August through September, heavy-shouldered cohos return to spawn, running a gauntlet of drift boats. Daily jet service from Seattle means that this river is as accessible to visitors as it is to Alaskans, and this shows in the number of fishers arriving on every flight when the runs are at their peaks. But the fish are there, with a return of as many as eight thousand steelhead, ranging up to about twenty pounds. It also has good fishing for kings, sockeyes, and cohos during the summer months. Those venturing into this country during the autumn storms will also find a smaller fall run of steelhead, but these fish are overwhelmed by the huge number of silvers that arrive around the end of August.

The Situk is small and clear, only twenty-two miles long. Easily accessible from Yakutat, it can be floated or fished on foot. A bridge over the river about nine miles from town allows access to the upper stretches and provides a put-in for the fourteen-mile float to the mouth. Trails lead both up- and downstream from the bridge, providing fishing for the nonboating angler. There is good fly fishing near the mouth, and a trail leads upstream for a couple miles, opening up some of the best areas for fishing from the bank. Be prepared for fishers who will simply park on a hole all day, every day. The traditional courtesy of working down through a hole so another angler can cover the water behind you has not taken hold in many Alaskan waters.

The most prominent feature of the Situk is the massive numbers of snags and sweepers. As with many Alaskan rivers, the banks are constantly undercut and the big spruce that line the river sometimes block the entire stream. The biggest problem is that the trees provide great shelter for the fish, which will lie just behind a current-breaking snag, making them nearly invulnerable to a fly caster. If you do manage to get a fly to them, they will invariably take you right into the maze of branches, creating a cat's cradle with your expensive fly line. The crystal-clear water of the Situk provides exciting sight fishing, but it also means that the fish are particularly wary, especially if the sun is shining.

The weather in Yakutat is infamously bad; it's one of the wettest places in the state. Spring steelheaders may find themselves sandwiched between towering snowdrifts lining both banks, with sleet flying horizontally up the river. It's cold, but the sight of a dozen big steelhead lying on the bottom of a run will go a long way toward taking the chill off.

The Situk gets most of the press, but other rivers near Yakutat also provide very good fishing for salmon, although unfortunately, not for steelhead. The Italio River, only twenty-five air miles from Yakutat, is a beautiful clear-water stream—well, streams, actually. It has three branches, the Old, Middle, and New Italio. The stream channels shift course on a regular basis, but all of them host runs of trophy-size cohos.

It's the fall rains in September that bring the fish into these systems, so go prepared for heavy weather. For those looking for more modest fishing—and better weather—the Italio has cutthroat in May and September and Dolly Varden from July through September.

The Akwe River, a few miles south of the Italio, affords an opportunity to fish for some large sea-run cutthroat, as well as silvers. The main river is glacial and often too silty for decent fishing, but the clearwater tributaries provide some fine fly rodding. The East Alsek provides good fishing for kings in late May and early June, with the fishing concentrated at the mouth. It also has a healthy run of sockeyes, which arrive several weeks after they show up in the other rivers in the area. Look for them in late July. Additionally, it has a good run of silvers and the only chums in the area. The Doame River, near the Alsek, is an untouched beauty with fine fishing for silvers in the fall.

The area north of Yakutat, known as the Lost Coast, burst onto the angling scene a few years ago. It remains the domain of the adventurous fly fisher. Bordering the edge of Wrangell–St. Elias National Park, the Lost Coast lies between the storm-tossed Gulf of Alaska and the massive Bagley Ice Field. It is tough country, with commensurate rewards for those anglers who love tangling with big silvers. These rivers not only hold a lot of fish, but also are among the largest in the state.

This is an area of stunning beauty, at least when the skies are clear enough to get a glimpse of the ice-clad peaks, which include some of the highest in North America. The Wrangells and the St. Elias Range trap the moisture-laden storms, and the result is predictable. One glacier, the Malaspina, is larger than Rhode Island. Although the melting ice creates huge silt-laden rivers, there are enough clear streams to make this a hidden treasure for coho fishers.

The reputation of this area was not made on the fish, however, but the method of fishing. It was on these rivers that George Davis and a few others pioneered the use of skated dry flies for cohos—one of the most exciting fisheries available. Articles began popping up in national magazines describing a hitherto unknown area where big silvers would attack surface patterns. The first pattern to be used successfully was a hot pink deer-hair bug known as a Pink Pollywog, and the technique soon became known as wogging. Even for Alaskans jaded about catching salmon, the sight of a big male coho engulfing a dry fly will be burned into the memory.

The most well-known river is the Tsiu, a small, clear-water stream about halfway between Cordova and Yakutat. Heavily braided, the Tsiu runs through an area of sand dunes, a far cry from the terrain surrounding most salmon streams. The river is only a couple feet deep, and it broadens and slows as it reaches tidewater. The smooth, moderate current and shallow depth make it perfect for wogging the huge runs of silvers that enter the system from late August through September. The runs are huge, up to two hundred thousand fish in a good year, making the Tsiu one of the most productive streams of its size in Alaska.

The Tsiu is not the only great coho fishery on this stretch of coast. The nearby Kiklukh and the remote Kaliakh can both be great as well. These rivers require gravel-bar landings, though, and the fishing peaks during the fall storms. Closer to Yakutat, the streams of Icy Bay present wonderful opportunities for skating drys. Icy Bay is the spectacular setting for George Davis's lodge, where I discovered just how much fun it is to take cohos on the surface.

There are more accessible fisheries near Cordova. The Eyak River and the Alaganik Slough system are road-accessible, although a boat will help get you to the best spots. Both are partially glacial but have clear-water tributaries and sloughs that hold congregations of fish. Sockeyes, cutthroat, and Dollies are present, but cohos are the principal target species.

Although most people visiting this area will remain within the road systems of Cordova and Yakutat, it's the remote sections that make the Lost Coast so special. This is truly wild country, where you feel as if you have stepped back two centuries. The streams, cutting through black-sand beaches to empty into the Gulf of Alaska, provide perhaps the best coho fishing in the state. Bear and wolf tracks are common; footprints are not. With the Wrangell–St. Elias Range as a background, it would be hard to find a more breathtaking fishery.

17

TAKING COHOS
ON THE SURFACE
with George Davis

The small bush plane loaded with groceries and dog food sat on over-size "tundra tires," designed for landing on beaches and gravel bars. It was a rare cloudless day in Yakutat, perfect for flying in to one of the most stunning spots in Alaska: Icy Bay. Framed against Mount St. Elias, North America's third-highest peak, the bay gets its name from the tidewater glaciers that wind down the mountain slopes. From the air, I could see glacial tendrils snaking out from the Bagley Ice Field, a vast sea of snow and ice. A line of blue-white icebergs marches down the bay's shoreline. The land is thick with spruce and alder, and black-sand beaches mark the Pacific's edge. In spite of logging scars, I had that edge-of-the-world feeling as the plane prepared to touch down on a long beach just inside the bay. It's easy to see why this area is often referred to as the Lost Coast.

A short distance from the beach, George Davis's Icy Bay Lodge takes full advantage of the area's beauty. It wasn't the scenery that brought George here, though. It was the huge runs of silver salmon that feed along its edges and ultimately flood into its short streams. This is classic coho country. Massive storm-built beaches slow and channel the water flooding through the coastal marshes, creating ideal rearing habitat for coho fry. Behind the beaches, the rivers have a slow and even flow that creates perfect opportunities for George's specialty—fishing dry flies for big cohos.

George's operation in Icy Bay is relatively new, but he has been guiding in this area since 1975. He grew up in the Chilkat Valley, near

Haines, and began fishing commercially at an early age, earning a living seining salmon, long-lining, and flying spotter planes for the herring fishery. George was one of the first people to take clients in to the Tsiu River, where he began experimenting with what was then a new technique, skating huge, hot pink deer-hair flies in front of pods of cohos. The Tsiu is now a well-known and heavily used destination, but the same techniques George developed there have proved successful in Icy Bay and every other coho stream that has the right topography.

It was the end of August when I flew in to Icy Bay, and the silvers were just starting to arrive. An abnormally warm summer had delayed the beginning of the run, which usually starts about August 20. Typical of my timing, the major surge of fish hit two days after I left, with anglers reporting twenty-fish days and lots of surface action. The peak of the run is ordinarily around September 10. It then tapers off until October 1, when a second surge of fish hits, and fresh salmon continue to come in throughout the month. These are not small fish. George's biggest was a twenty-four-pound, four-ounce monster, and he usually gets about fifteen fish a year that run from eighteen to twenty-two pounds. Every year, fish over twenty pounds are taken on skated drys. The big males have such heavy shoulders that they are referred to as "whalebacks."

George fishes three types of water from his lodge, conditions that are similar to those found in many parts of the Lost Coast, Kodiak, and Southeast. The techniques he uses are readily transferable to those areas.

The first type of water is the river mouths and coastal lagoons. The streams along the Lost Coast typically flow through grassy marshes and then form lagoons behind the barrier beaches. Fishing at the mouths of these rivers is tide-dependent. The salmon come up on the rising tide, holding right on the seams that mark the freshwater boundary. As the tide starts to ebb, the fish push across into the shallow water and begin heading upstream. They can be aggressive when they first come across, but quickly get spooky in the unfamiliar environment. George likes to fish the first pool above salt water, where the fish hold while they acclimate. They can be voracious under those circumstances.

Silvers sometimes wait several tide cycles before they move into fresh water, particularly if the weather is sunny. Those fish that do not move into the river drop back with the tide. These fish still continue to feed and can be taken on baitfish patterns as the tide falls.

The second productive area is the salt chucks at the outlets of the tiny creeks that drain pothole lakes. It's difficult to believe that a stream that may be only a couple feet wide and a few inches deep will support a run of fifteen-pound fish, but the deeper pools and lakes that form in the flat landscape often provide enough water to sustain them. The creeks themselves are too small to fish, but the flats in front of them often attract salmon.

"They get that taste of fresh water and stay there. One of my clients took eighteen fish one morning in front of that creek," George told me, pointing to a tiny rivulet of water draining across the beach. "You'll see jumpers all along it when the run is peaking."

The third type of water is the large tidal flats that develop behind some of the spits and points. There the salmon feed in water only a couple feet deep, looking for sand lance and other baitfish and providing some of the most exciting sight fishing available. On a calm day, you can see small pods of cohos slowly cruising the flats, their dorsal fins projecting out of the water. Silent wakes, shoulder bulges, and swirls mark their presence. The similarity to fishing for tailing bonefish is immediate, and the same amount of caution and careful stalking are required. The one difference is that bonefish won't hit a skated dry fly.

Regardless of the type of water fished, George recommends an 8- or 9-weight rod. For dry flies, George has his clients use a tapered leader from 7 ½ to 12 feet long, with a 12- or 16-pound tippet. The flies are bulky, so a stiff butt section will help turn them over in the wind. In deeper water, he uses a minitip with 4 feet of level tippet. Longer leaders, lighter tippets, and even fluorocarbon may be necessary in low, clear water or on bright days when the fish are particularly spooky.

Topwater flies are designed to attract attention. Not only do they skate and gurgle, but they also are invariably tied in the brightest colors possible. Hot pink and chartreuse are the two favorites, and a bit of flash is usually added. The classic coho dry fly is the Pink Pollywog, tied from hot pink deer hair, which was the first pattern to achieve consistent success. Its use is so widespread that the technique is often referred to as wogging. In spite of the fly's effectiveness, George doesn't recommend it, for a reason that will become immediately obvious the first time you use one—it's miserable to cast.

A Dahlberg Slider, tied in bright colors, often with a contrasting ring of white just in front of the collar, is a bit more aerodynamic. This is essentially a traditional Dahlberg Diver, tied with a bit less slope on the top and collar, which helps keep it on the surface, and a tail of marabou and Flashabou.

After a couple days of fishing, my favorite pattern turned out to be a foam and Crystal Chenille fly that goes by various names, including the Techno Spanker, Hot Lips, and Coho Seizure. The fly floats well, casts easily, and is quick to tie. George also had a selection of poppers made from rubber sandals, with marabou and flash in the tails. Occasionally a blue-and-yellow or purple deer-hair slider will work well. All of these flies should be tied on wide-gape hooks, such a Mustad 3366. Bass stinger hooks have a wide gape, but they are too light to consistently hold fish this big.

Although the area is famed for its topwater action, fishing deep, not surprisingly, is more effective. For those stretches where you need to get to the bottom, George suggests an intermediate sinking-tip or a Teeny minitip. A heavy sinker, up to a 300-grain Teeny or the equivalent, can also be useful, particularly when fishing the mouths of the rivers during a rapidly falling tide.

George's favorite fly is one he developed himself and of which he is justifiably proud, the Davis Spanker. It's a simple creation with a body of Krystal Chenille and a pulsating tail of Flashabou and Krystal Flash. It's a world-record holder, and I can attest to its effectiveness. It has become my go-to fly for cohos wherever I find them. Tied in hot pink, chartreuse, or a combination of the two, it has the color and flash that trigger coho strikes. It is also tied in black, as cohos can be even more fickle than steelhead in their color demands.

Other productive streamer patterns include the ubiquitous Egg-Sucking Leech in black and purple, Popsicles, and the Karluk Flash Fly. Bunny Leeches in fuchsia, black, and purple are good, as are Articulated Leeches. Teeny Nymphs can be effective. In the salt, including the salt chuck and the incoming tide in the river mouths, George's clients have good luck with typical saltwater baitfish patterns such as ALFs, Deceivers, and Clousers.

But it's the surface action that gets everyone's attention. The interest of even the most jaded coho fisher will be rejuvenated by catching salmon on top. Few freshwater opportunities are more exciting than watching a big buck coho move up behind your fly, stick his nose out of the water, and engulf it. Catching them on top requires certain conditions, however. The holding water should be about two to four feet deep and have a shallow gradient, creating a smooth surface with a moderate current. Cohos will hit a surface fly in stillwater, including salt water, but skating doesn't work very well in fast currents. George qualifies this, though, by saying that when the fish are moving up through the riffles, water spraying as they splash forward, you can sometimes get one to hit a popper dropped right on its nose and pulled up in front of it. George says these fish will continue to hit surface flies all the way up to the spawning grounds, which basically means that it's worth trying a topwater fly any time you find fish schooled up in the right river flow.

The best fishing is when the fish are schooled up. Silvers often hold high in the water column, their backs so close to the surface that their dorsals stick up like tiny sails. They are particularly vulnerable to a surface fly in those situations. When I was there, with the run just beginning, we had our best luck with the fish that were just coming into the river, skating flies in the last part of the current before it hit the high tide's confluence line. As the tide began to ebb, the fish came across the line, and in spite of the skinny water and bright sun, some of them were surprisingly aggressive.

Silvers love those barely moving seams, eddies, and back channels collectively referred to as "frog water." When we found a bunch, George had me cast the fly right in front of the fish so that I was stripping it away from them. Silvers, like tarpon, don't like to be attacked by anything, even something as small as a size 2 popper. If you have spotted fish, you need to put the fly close to them. Although silvers will follow a fly for a long distance, they won't move very far to get to it.

"Use a steady, moderately fast popping action," George advises. "Keep stripping when you see the wake coming behind the fly, but when you see that beak come out of the water to take it, you need to hesitate just slightly. If you continue stripping as the fish goes for the fly, it will often turn away at the last second, and you won't get anything but a boil behind the fly. Remember, the fish will be coming right at you, and it's very easy to pull the fly right out of its mouth. You have to give the fish time to close its mouth and turn in order to set the hook."

With silvers, though, nothing works all the time and everything works some of the time. "If you aren't getting strikes, change the strip speed. If that doesn't work, change color. I usually use a pink, chartreuse, orange, dark sequence," George says.

If the surface action is slow, go deep. Although silvers will hang high in the water in areas of slow current, they are most likely to be right on the bottom of the faster water, and you need to get down to them. George likes to cast the fly at a forty-five-degree angle downstream and let it dead drift and sink. When the fly reaches the end and starts to swing, use a short, fast strip, then let it stop and flutter back. Keep repeating the strip-and-flutter pattern until the fly is hanging directly below you.

One of the best places to intercept silvers is right at the mouth of a river. Start at the beginning of the flood tide, and as the fish come in, continue to move up with the tide, fishing right at the current line. As the tide starts to ebb, you can move back down, but bear in mind that many fish will move into the river as the tide begins to drop.

Fish will also hold at the confluence of two streams. Fish the seam between the two currents, using the same forty-five-degree cast and dead drift technique. If one of the streams is silty or colored up, the fish will often hold just on the edge of the dirty water, so work the strip-and-flutter retrieve along that edge.

Light is a critical factor in the success rate for silvers. They are very sensitive to bright sunshine and get spooky and close-mouthed. The best days are overcast and rainy, when the fish don't feel as vulnerable. Although it's certainly possible to have good fishing in nice weather, you usually have to work harder.

When the silvers arrive in force, there are too many for even the hungriest meat fisher. Silvers are surprisingly fragile, and good catch-and-release skills are important to avoid killing fish. That requires more than barbless hooks and strong tippets. Get the fish in as quickly as possible to avoid exhausting them and creating a dangerous buildup of lactic acid.

This means keeping pressure on them at all times so they can't rest. Jumps and long runs will wear them out, so you want to force the fish to fight. The best way to do that is to work them from the side, with the rod tip low, so you are pulling their head sideways. Follow them down the bank so that you stay even with the fish and are fighting them across the current. The worst technique is to simply stand upstream and hold your rod high. All the fish has to do is set its fins and you are just fighting the current. Force the fish into the bank so it will feel the sand under its belly and panic. Just be prepared to let it run when that happens. As soon as it pauses, start fighting it again so it doesn't have time to recuperate. Like the difference between running sprints and running a mile, you want the fish to fight you anaerobically rather than pace itself for the long haul.

When you land the fish, keep it in the water to release it. Never pick up a fish that you intend to release by the gills or tail. Although this is useful for landing salmon destined for the grill, it will break the cartilage in the spine, and the fish likely won't survive. The best way to land a silver is probably with a Boga Grip, which will allow you to control the fish and, if you want, weigh it at the same time.

George says his clients regularly make three common mistakes. Anglers often want to wade into the river, which spooks the fish. Unless you need to get into the water to reach the holding lies, you are far better off keeping your feet dry or at least staying very close to the bank. The second mistake is letting a hooked fish take control of the fight. These are big, strong fish, and if you give them time to rest or let them get downstream of you, where you are just pulling against the current, you are more likely to lose the fish and will certainly do more damage to it. The third problem is the tendency to begin stripping the fly as soon as it hits the water. Let the fly dead drift down through the current and sink to the proper depth before you start the retrieve.

George has developed some very efficient techniques for taking big cohos from the waters that surround his lodge. These same techniques can be equally effective in a number of other areas. The islands of the Kodiak archipelago have similar flats and salt chucks, and the silvers there undoubtedly will respond to the same skated drys or slowly stripped Davis Spankers. Anglers throughout the state have found that George's topwater tactics for silvers work anywhere you find fish stacked in water with a smooth, even flow.

Although George's techniques may work elsewhere, no other place in the state has the same magic mixture of overwhelming beauty, complete remoteness, and big silvers. If you're looking for a true Alaskan adventure and some great fishing, Icy Bay Lodge has to be high on the list of perfect destinations.

18

SOUTHEAST ALASKA

Alaska's southeastern panhandle, which Alaskans just call Southeast, is a dramatic landscape six hundred miles long, rich with marine life. Narrow fjords cut into steep, heavily forested islands, ending in tiny coves with water that is perfectly clear and calm, the reflections of the surrounding mountains broken only by the disturbance of hundreds of pink salmon milling just beyond the outlet of their natal stream, the taste of home in their mouths. The Tongass National Forest of Southeast is truly one of the most beautiful places on earth.

The overriding factors in understanding Southeast are geography and climate. Steep mountainous islands, some of them very large, lie off the equally rugged coast. Pounded by the North Pacific weather systems, the Tongass is the largest temperate rain forest in the world. Up to seventy inches of rain fall every year in some areas. The result is a huge number of short, small streams plunging through heavy forest. The storm-tossed outer coast lies exposed to open ocean, but the sheltered inner water, including the beautiful Inside Passage, is well protected. The area has classic maritime climate, with weather that is mild and cool. Rain and fog are interspersed with periods of brilliant sunshine.

Steep slopes, deep straits and bays, and abundant precipitation have created one of the richest and most exciting ecosystems in the world. It's not unusual to see brown bears digging for clams along the beaches or sea lions cruising the shore. Humpback whales, ravenous from a winter's fast off the coast of Hawaii, gorge on the schools of herring that congregate here. Bald eagles are everywhere, and the cry of gulls is a constant. There's much more to fishing in Southeast than just the fish, but they are there too.

This is world-class fishing water, teeming with salmon, steelhead, and coastal cutthroat. But it's almost entirely a saltwater troll fishery. That's unfortunate, because a fly fisher can find a vast country of streams and coastal creeks that are rarely fished. There are no large destination rivers here, but great fly-rod fishing can be found in the salt chucks and river mouths. Small tannin-stained streams, choked with moss-covered blowdowns, hide runs of spring steelhead. It's rare to see another angler, except on those streams in close proximity to one of the dozen towns and villages scattered throughout the area.

Access is far more problematic than technique. Although substantial areas of the Tongass have been clear-cut, and taxpayer-subsidized logging roads lead to a number of small streams, getting a vehicle to most of these roads is impossible, and the logging has done so much damage to the watersheds that the survival of many of these fisheries is at risk. Southeast can prove an enigma to anglers habituated to roadside fishing.

Fortunately, there are other ways to find that combination of fish, rain-forest beauty, and seclusion unique to Southeast. Fishers with a sense of adventure can have a water taxi deliver them, complete with sea kayaks, to a remote Forest Service cabin. Others can fish off a mother ship that explores the coves and bays. Guides are available in most towns and can provide day trips to pursue whichever species of fish is at its peak.

The Forest Service cabin option is an ideal way to experience this area. They are clean, dry, and comfortable and provide welcome shelter from the frequent rains and occasional wandering bear. A small boat will provide transportation to likely fishing spots and a platform from which to cast. You're on your own here, but if you've timed it right and the salmon are starting to stage outside the creek mouths, a guide is unnecessary—and if the fish haven't arrived, a guide won't help.

For those who want a bit more luxury and the help of someone who knows the local waters, a mother ship will put you on fish. Be careful about the skipper, though. Fly fishing is new and still unusual in this area, and most of the captains focus solely on deep-water fishing with trolling gear or halibut rods.

A few guides scattered throughout the area specialize in fly fishing, and they are certainly your best bet for catching fish. They are particularly good if you have a short stay in one of the towns of Southeast, because they can get you into a day's fishing with a short boat run. Most have some facility for overnighting on the water.

The myriad of streams provide spawning for salmon and steelhead, with pinks and silvers being the most abundant. Steelhead ascend the rivers in spring, but they are summer-run fish and drop back out of the rivers immediately after spawning. Most of these streams have returns of only a hundred fish or so. The beginning of the runs, which last only a few weeks, varies from stream to stream. Finding steelhead in Southeast requires a guide, local knowledge, or a lot of luck. On the other hand, when it works, it's an experience that will stick in your mind for life. Tiny plunge pools, often overlain with a tangle of fallen moss-covered trees, may hold half a dozen bright steelhead. Hooking them is one thing, but landing them is another. You won't catch many fish in these waters unless you're willing to climb, crawl, and scramble.

Steelhead may be difficult, but pink salmon can be almost too easy. Massive schools stage in the coves and bays into which their spawning streams empty. This can be a fish-on-every-cast scenario. Pink salmon begin to deteriorate as soon as they taste fresh water, and as a consequence, they are much maligned in Alaska. But they can be a lot of fun if you can find them while they are still in the salt and even more fun on a dry fly. They are also an ideal fish for kids—eager to hit, scrappy, and prolific. Casting from shore is possible in some places, but a small boat that allows you to get fifty yards offshore is a big help.

Cohos are the primary target species inmost of Southeast. They are particularly adapted to the small coastal streams that dot the islands, and the area has a couple thousand such streams that host at least a few spawning cohos. Many of these creeks are barely big enough for the returning fish to make it past the high-tide mark. Nevertheless, coho mill about at the outlets of these tiny streams, the barest scent of fresh water in their noses.

Even though most of the fishing is in the salt water, run timing is as critical in Southeast as anywhere else. The silvers generally run late in the year, during September and October. There is an earlier run around Wrangell, though. The fish return from their feeding grounds in the

Gulf of Alaska and begin to stage near their natal streams several weeks before they are ready to enter fresh water. These fish are actively feeding and will hit baitfish imitations such as Clousers, Lefty's Deceivers, and the various epoxy-headed patterns.

The most difficult part of chasing offshore cohos with a fly rod is finding the fish. The same techniques described for saltwater fishing in Resurrection Bay apply here, but local knowledge is always best. If you're on your own, look for the types of water described in those chapters and you'll have a good start. Although you won't find a lot of opportunities to fish surface flies for cohos in Southeast, take a few along in case you find fish in the shallows.

Cutthroat trout are perhaps the most ubiquitous sport fish species in the southern part of the panhandle. They are all coastal cutthroat, but some of them spend their entire lives in the freshwater lakes and ponds of the Tongass. There are large populations of anadromous cutthroat throughout most of the area, although their migratory patterns can make them maddeningly elusive.

Cutthroat spend their winters in fresh water, migrating out to sea in late spring and returning during the early fall. They are opportunistic feeders, but in areas with salmon, which includes all but the smallest creeks, they focus on eggs, alevins, and fry. Nevertheless, they will readily hit nymphs and dry flies in fresh water. These are not large fish by Alaskan standards, usually running ten to sixteen inches. Strangely enough, the largest are not the sea-run cutts, but those that live in the lakes.

Cutts can be found near most of the cities of Southeast, either in the mountain lakes or along the coastal streams. A fair amount of fishing for them can be had near Ketchikan, particularly in the Misty Fjords area. The area lakes hold some large trout, and there is some fishing for them along the road system. Petersburg and Wrangell offer fishing in the innumerable creeks and along the rocky coastline.

Dolly Varden are also found in most of the coastal streams of the Tongass. As you move farther north toward Juneau, they become more common than the cutthroat. Like the cutts, they migrate in and out of the fresh water and are best targeted near the mouths of the creeks. They are not large, but they can make for good light-tackle fishing in the early season, when there are no other opportunities. Luke Woodruff has figured out the secrets of targeting Dollies, and the next chapter will get you well on your way to success.

Southeast is not a common destination for a fly rodder planning an Alaskan vacation. The area has no rainbow trout, fly fishing for king salmon is very limited, and few guides and lodges cater to fly fishers. Nevertheless, you'll find some spectacularly good fishing, the scenery and wildlife are stunning, and the cost can be far less than any of the other true wilderness destinations. Whether you're a cruise ship passenger spending the day in Juneau, a sea kayaker looking for a wilderness expedition, or one of a lucky group with a reservation for a Forest Service cabin, take your fly rod along. You may discover some of the most enjoyable fishing you'll ever experience.

19

FISHING
THE RAIN FOREST
with Luke Woodruff

Fishing may be the lifeblood of Southeast, but a fly rod will get you a lot of strange looks on most of the docks. Only a handful of local anglers have spent the time necessary to explore the full range of fly-fishing opportunities here. One of them is Luke Woodruff.

Luke grew up in Juneau and, at twenty-nine, has been guiding for the past eight years. Luke has focused exclusively on fly fishing, and it has given him an insight into the fishery that belies his youth. He owns Sea Runner Guide Service, operating a twenty-foot aluminum skiff, and focuses on the estuaries and river mouths near Juneau. Luke provides one of the few opportunities for cruise ship passengers touring the Inside Passage to satisfy their lust to get a fly rod in hand—and if you didn't bring yours, Luke can provide one. This part of the state has no rainbows, but it has plenty of Dolly Varden, chums, pink and silver salmon, cutthroat, and for a lucky few, steelhead.

Luke's guiding season begins about May 1, when the Dollies begin to migrate out of the lakes where they spent the winter. They drop down to the estuaries and creek mouths, where they feed heavily on the newly hatched chum and pink fry. The Dollies will stay near the mouths of the creeks, rarely leaving the bays or venturing more than half a mile upstream. From April until the end of June, the Dollies remain congregated in the intertidal zone, and the fishing is dependent on the tides. The fishing varies from creek to creek, with some best on a rising tide and others hitting their peak on the ebb. Some estuaries fish better with lots of water, and others improve as the flats begin to go dry. Each has its own schedule. The one constant is that the fish like some current, and the fishing almost always dies down dramatically on the slack tides, both high and low.

Having said that the fish feed best when there is some current, Luke points out that they don't like to hold in places with a lot of current. The fry prefer the slower edges, and that's where the Dollies are found. Luke looks for them in the eddies and deeper water. They also often hold along the seams between currents of two different speeds. A lot of the fry move in the upper water column, and the Dollies like to trap them against the surface. In many creeks, it's common to see them slashing at the trapped baitfish. "Those aren't fish rising to dry flies," Luke says. "They're chasing fry, and you need to be throwing small streamers."

Most of the fishing is done by wading, but going deep is counterproductive. "If you're standing in knee-deep water, you're probably standing where you should be fishing," Luke says. "The fish will often school up right at the upper end of the tide, just as it meets the fresh water. You need to follow the tideline up to keep with the fish, but they are very competitive then, and the fishing can be very good."

Don't expect Alaskan-size fish in these small creeks. Most run fourteen to seventeen inches, with an occasional fish running as big as twenty-one to twenty-three inches. Luke's biggest Dolly was a twenty-six-incher. He likes to use a 6-weight rod for Dollies. Depending on the conditions, he uses either a floating line or an intermediate sinking-tip. He ties a simple 9-foot tapered leader with three sections: 15-, 10-, and 6-pound. If silvers are in the water, as is the case later in the summer, he will go to a 10-pound tippet.

For flies, he uses natural-colored Clouser Minnows, tied in white and olive, white and gray, or white and brown. He likes size 4 hooks; size 2s will occasionally kill small fish, and size 6s sometimes get inhaled. The fry tend to stay near the surface, so he keeps his fly swimming shallow. He likes to vary the retrieve but starts with a quick, short strip. Flies that move too slowly get too many refusals. "You want the fly to move just fast enough that the fish doesn't have time to think about it," he says.

In early July, the Dollies begin to move back up into the creeks, following the salmon. There are no eggs in the water this early, and Luke continues to use small streamers. He fishes the holes and uses more weight, working the fly near the bottom. Nymphs can also be productive as the salmon begin to build their redds and stir up the bottom. Although many people use strike indicators for this fishing, as well as for fishing egg patterns a little later in the season, Luke prefers to simply high-stick the fly, keeping it bouncing along the bottom on a tight line.

Once the salmon begin to spawn, Luke fishes for Dollies with Glo-Bugs, Battle Creeks, and flesh flies. He uses beads only as a last resort. The Dollies show a marked preference for chum eggs, and fishing behind the pinks is much less productive. By late season, the Dollies have moved onto their own spawning grounds and into the lakes and are very difficult to find.

Dollies are the focus of the early season, but by about June 20, the salmon start arriving at the creek mouths. The first to show are the chums—tough, heavy-bodied sluggers. Fishing starts in the estuaries where the salmon stage, following the tideline in and out as they prepare to move into the streams. They are at their most aggressive when they first hit the mouths of the creeks, but according to Luke, unlike chums in some other areas of the state, they can be finicky about flies and retrieves. Still, as for all chums, pink is the color of choice. Luke likes two flies particularly, the Sparkle Shrimp and a simple tie he calls Pink Dynamite.

The pink salmon show up about five days behind the chums, and for a time you don't know what you will hook—a fourteen-inch Dolly, a four-pound pink, or a ten-pound chum. The first few pinks of the season are always incidental to the other fish, but once they show up in force, you can stand in one spot all day and catch as many as your arm can handle. Luke fishes pinks until the cohos show up, with a few late pinks showing up as late as mid-August.

Pinks will hit the same Clousers used for Dollies, but the flies typically used for chums work better. Luke likes a more active retrieve than he uses for chums—short, quick strips or two quick strips and a pause. Pencil Poppers also work well for pinks.

Coho fishing begins in earnest about the first of September and peaks about the middle of the month. There is some fishing in the estuaries and creek mouths, but Luke much prefers fishing in the rivers. He looks for fish in the slow, deep pools. Like silvers everywhere, these fish don't hold in fast water. The creeks of Southeast are full of logjams—this is rain forest, after all—and the cohos love them. The current digs out deep pools below the logs, the water slows, and the tangles provide cover and darkness. Count on losing a lot of fish.

Catching silvers on these rivers means going deep. A lot of anglers use floating lines and split shot, but Luke says that most of the time the flies are going over the fish's head. He likes very heavy lines, preferably with interchangeable heads. His usual system for silvers is to cut a 750-grain Deep Water Express into segments short enough to be cast. Leaders may be as short as 2 feet and never longer than four. This system is pretty much limited to roll casting, but these streams have so much brush that a backcast is usually impossible anyway.

Luke casts across, quartering either up or down, depending on the current. He lets the fly swing with little or no added motion. "Stripping causes the fly to ride up, and you need to be right on the bottom. At most, I will give it an intermittent strip, just enough to make the fly twitch. Really, it's just swinging."

Big flies are the norm here. Luke likes size 2 or larger, often going to 1/0 or 2/0 hooks. "With all of the snags in the river, you have to be able to control the fish. Smaller flies will pull out." Purple Bunny Leeches and pink-and-white Clousers are his go-to flies. Chartreuse can be good, and if the water is stained, he likes darker patterns. Although Luke likes bright colors for silvers, he ties with only a limited amount of flash. He says he's seen fish flee from Flash Flies. He usually adds dumbbell eyes or some weight but relies on the heavy lines to do most of the work getting the fly deep.

Unlike coho fisheries in some other parts of the state, Juneau has little in the way of dry-fly action. Luke carries a few hard-bodied Pencil Poppers, though, and if he can find fish holding in slow water no deeper than three feet, he will give them a shot.

Pinks, chums, and silvers are the basis of Luke's salmon fishing, but a few lucky anglers get a shot at king salmon. Although kings are sometimes an incidental catch in other saltwater fisheries, this area provides one of the few opportunities to target them in the ocean with a fly rod. The secret is a hatchery on the north end of Douglas Island that produces kings. The fish return from about June 10 through 25 and can be ambushed just outside the estuary near the mouth of the creek. The kings require a flood tide to come up over the shelf that has developed at the outflow of the river. By anchoring in the seaweed just off the shelf, you can cast to fish on the rising tide. Once the flats are flooded, the fish scatter, and it's time to pull up and go home. It is only a four-hour window, and the odds are poor, so Luke will fish it only on request. But if you hook a king in salt water on a fly rod, it will have made the gamble worthwhile.

Luke likes a 10-weight rod with an intermediate shooting taper or slow-sinking line, although a sinking-tip will also work. Flies are big, size 3/0 and 5 or 6 inches long. He prefers Seaducers tied in hot pink, with red or orange as the contrast color. They are tied with heavy bead-chain or dumbbell eyes, in a variety of weights. You need to change the amount of weight as the tide moves in, usually about every half hour. If you can't find or tie the fly, Luke says that plastic trolling Hoochies, available at every sporting-goods store in Juneau, will work as well.

For some fly anglers, the ultimate prize in fishing the rain-forest creeks of the Tongass is steelhead. Finding these scarce and elusive fish is so problematic that Luke doesn't guide for steelhead—but he loves to fish for them. There are so many small creeks tumbling out of the forest that the fish are scattered everywhere. Many streams may have a return of only a couple dozen fish; others may have a couple thousand.

These are all spring-run fish, and they begin to return in mid-April, with the first fish showing on the outside of Baranof or Chichigof Islands. The run lasts until June, but the fish don't dawdle in fresh water. They move into the rivers, pair up, spawn, and drop back out in short order. Finding them is more like hunting than fishing. The fish are so scarce that it's essentially all sight fishing. You need to be able to spot the fish hunkered down in the creeks to have a shot at them.

Luke fishes a floating line with an indicator. With fresh fish, he likes a small, brightly colored nymph, Woolly Bugger, or Glo-Bug. As the season progresses, he goes to more subtle colors, using olive, brown, or black on fish that have been in the river long enough to darken up. The nymphing is all dead drift, but he says that if he gets refusals, he can sometimes tempt them by swinging a Clouser Minnow in front of them on a tight line.

Not many anglers choose Southeast for their Alaskan fly-fishing destination, but the region offers more opportunities than most people realize—and the side benefits are unparalleled. Humpback whales, sea lions, and orcas, as well as the spectacular scenery, make for an unforgettable trip. Combine that with sea kayaking, a Forest Service cabin, or a day with Luke Woodruff, and Southeast will rank high on your all-time list of favorite fishing spots.

PART V

TROPHIES AND TROUBLES: ENSURING A SUCCESSFUL TRIP

The techniques described by the guides in this book are often unique to specific fisheries. But some of the things that you need to know are applicable statewide. Regardless of where you're going or what you're fishing for, the information in these last few chapters will help keep a smile on your face when things get tricky.

If you're new to Alaska, you probably need to learn the techniques it takes to control and land fish that are big enough to test the limits of your tackle. Stories about the one that got away are never as good as the grip-and-grin photo hanging on your wall. Nanci Morris Lyon explains how to get that trophy in hand and, equally important, how to release it without injury.

Everyone is concerned about bears. They are a constant in Alaska, and good bear etiquette will make being around them safer, albeit more nerve-racking, than crossing a city street. The bears aren't the only difficulty, though. You will be fishing in subarctic or maritime conditions, and that means bugs and bad weather. The right gear will minimize the discomfort. Learning how to deal with these potential problems will go a long way toward making your trip more enjoyable.

Finally, a fly-fishing book would not be complete without a list of favorite flies. Knowing which flies work for the area, species, and time of year you plan to fish is important. It not only saves you money and tying time but helps ensure you don't end up on the river with only two copies of the killer fly.

Although the standard Alaskan patterns work well, every guide has a few of his own making that seem to outfish the ones you bought at the local fly shop. I have added the recipes for some of the flies that have been mentioned in this book. It's always worth having a few of these in your fly box.

20

LANDING BIG FISH:
The Techniques
of Nanci Morris Lyon

On many streams in the rest of the country, a twenty-inch rainbow would be the fish of a season. For fly fishers used to fourteen-inchers, landing a fish of that size poses a significant challenge. When they suddenly find themselves on an Alaskan stream where twenty inches is the average and a two-footer is a daily possibility, the habits learned on the Delaware or Madison are simply inadequate. Far too many visitors leave Alaska with tales of the ones that got away—and those long-distance releases are usually a result of operator error. If you want to be able to consistently land large fish, you need to master the techniques required to control and quickly tire them.

Few people have as much experience with large fish, particularly large rainbows, as Nanci Morris Lyon. She has helped her clients land an amazingly high number of trophies. Nanci has some helpful advice on what to do when you suddenly realize that the fish you traveled to Alaska for has just eaten your fly.

Getting the hook in is the first order of business. "It's important to use a strip strike, rather than attempting to set the hook by raising the rod tip," Nanci says. "The rod is simply too flexible, and you lose too much power. Give a firm, swift pull with the line hand, but be prepared to turn the fish loose to run as soon as you have driven the hook home. Big fish are usually going to make a long run as soon as they realize that they are hooked. Lift your rod high to get as much line off the water as possible, and let them go. Don't try to stop them on that initial run. I see clients begin to panic when the backing starts heading out the guides, and I just tell them, 'That's the reason you put it on your reel.' Let the fish use up all of its reserve oxygen on that first dash. You don't want to even try to control the fish on the initial run, but you need to be careful about letting it create a belly in the line. A long fly line in heavy current will cause enough drag to pull the hook out or break the fish off. High-sticking the fish on that first run helps prevent that problem."

When the fish has hit the end of its initial run, you need to take the fight to the fish. Keep the pressure on constantly. Letting a big fish rest allows it to fight longer, gives it a greater chance of coming unstuck, and is harder on it. Try to make the fish fight anaerobically, like a sprinter, instead of pacing itself, like a marathoner. You'll be surprised how fast you can whip a big fish if you never let it catch its breath—or whatever it is that fish do.

Once the first run is over and you've recaptured some line, lower the rod to the side. This pulls the fish's head sideways and forces it to fight with its body strength. If you have the rod high, the fish can set its pectoral fins and use the current to its advantage. And if you bring the fish to the surface and its head breaks the water, it will probably panic and start thrashing. That kind of violent action can be a disaster if the fish is on a short line.

Nanci is not a believer in flopping the rod back and forth. She says this causes the hook to open a hole and makes it easier for the fish to come unbuttoned. Pick a side and keep the rod there. The exception is if you turn the fish and are now pulling it directly from the front. If that happens, you need to change the angle of the line so you are continuing to put sideways pressure on it.

"It's important to know your equipment," Nanci says. "You need to understand how much pressure you can put on a fish without breaking it off. Too little pressure is almost as bad as too much, and it's a more common problem. I can land a fish in half the time it takes some of my clients, because I know exactly how much pressure I can put on the fish, and I never let up on it. I like to keep just enough drag on the reel to keep the spool from overrunning on the first run. After that, I use my hand to palm the reel, which gives me complete control over the amount of pressure I'm putting on the fish. If the fish jumps—and a twenty-two-incher will jump a lot—I like to immediately release the pressure. You don't need to bow to them like a tarpon, but you don't want them coming up hard on the line while they're in the air. And never try to change the drag on the reel while you're fighting a fish."

When you're fighting a big fish, you're often forced to follow it downstream in order to avoid trying to drag it back up against the current. It does little good to simply chase it, however. The purpose of following it is to keep the angle of attack right so that you are constantly putting pressure, preferably sideways, on the fish. When you follow a fish downstream, reel in as you move toward it, trying to hold the fish in position. The optimum distance from the fish is twenty or thirty feet—close enough to control it, but not so close that the sight of you puts the fish into a panic.

As you move downstream, have a plan for landing it in mind. "You should always look for an eddy or some slack water as a spot to land the fish," Nanci says. "It may be only a couple feet square, but you need to know where those spots are. Look downstream to see all your options. Once you get to the spot, hold the fish there. You want to be fighting the fish from an area where it's possible to land it."

If you're fighting the fish from a boat, use the boat to your advantage. You can usually maneuver the craft to keep the optimum angle on the fish. You need to keep the rod up if you're fighting from a boat, but the added mobility will let you keep the pressure on.

Nanci is a big advocate of rubber mesh nets, as they allow you to hold the fish in the water and control it without damaging its scales. Unfortunately, this type of web is available only in the large, heavy boat nets. If you're using a conventional net, make sure it has a shallow bag and soft mesh. Most nets available for wading anglers simply are not large enough to easily control Alaskan-size fish. Don't use that as a reason to buy one of the big salmon nets, though. They have a deep pocket, and the fish invariably tangle in the hard mesh and damage themselves.

Beaching a fish is often the best option, but your ability to do so is dependent on the terrain. Never drag a fish over the rocks. If the water is shallow and calm, you can often trap the fish with your net or feet without removing it from the water. If you're going to beach it, look for grass or sand. Walk backward up the beach so that you can keep the angle low enough to pull the fish steadily forward and not spook it. If you do it smoothly, you can usually slide the fish into water so shallow that it cannot get any power, with just its belly wet. At that point, quickly walk down, keeping the line tight, and you can control the fish without injuring it and often without dragging it onto the beach. If the fish is struggling too hard, try turning it upside down while it's still in the water. This tactic seems to disorient the fish and calm it down.

Big fish need to be handled carefully. Their weight alone can cause injury if they are picked up incorrectly. Put one hand behind the pectoral fins in order to balance the fish, and grasp the "wrist" just in front of the tail with your other hand. Be careful not to squeeze the fish, particularly with the hand in front, and avoid at all costs getting your fingers into the gills. Don't dangle a salmon by the "wrist" unless you plan to kill it; the body weight will cause the vertebrae to separate.

Minimize the time the fish is out of water. There's no reason to hold the fish in the air while your buddy fiddles with the camera. Besides, the best pictures are usually those with the fish still in the water, ready to be released, or at least with the water still dripping from the fish as you lift it. As Nanci puts it, "Hold your breath the entire time the fish is out of the water; after all, that's what the fish is doing."

Alaskan rainbows seem to recover more quickly than fish taken in warmer water, and they have a high survival rate if properly released. Don't use that as an excuse to just drop the fish back in the water, however. Big fish, particularly females of all species, need to be resuscitated until they are ready to go. Don't rely on the fact that the fish is making swimming motions. Their equilibrium and balance need to be restored before release, or you'll be chasing a belly-up fish as it floats downstream. Nanci suggests watching their eyes. If they're still glassy and not registering, the fish is not ready to take off on its own. Wait until the eyes brighten and drop down into their normal position before you release the fish.

Salmon, especially kings and silvers, are much more delicate than trout. This is particularly a problem with the females. Catch-and-release of salmon has a much higher mortality rate than is expected with trout, and you should keep this in mind when you think you've hit the mother lode. A little restraint may be necessary when you're catching salmon for sport. If you're releasing salmon, bring them in hot, keep them in the water, and use barbless hooks.

If the fish has swallowed the fly deep, don't put your fingers down its throat when trying to unhook it. Simply cut the leader and let the fish go. The hook will work its way out within a few days.

Nanci sees anglers make several common mistakes when they hook a big fish. The first is locking down on the fish during the initial run. Even if the fish doesn't break off, it won't exhaust itself, and the rest of the fight will be much harder and longer. Another mistake is following the fish too much as it runs downstream. Make the fish fight for that extra yardage. Find a spot of slack water, and fight the fish there. A third problem is failing to put enough pressure on the fish. You're not going to tire it out by just letting it hold in the current. Much worse, when you finally do get it in, you may have killed it because the lactic acid has built up for too long. Bring the fish in hot, and if you lose a few from putting too much pressure on them, that's okay; there are more fish in the river. Still another mistake is to fight the fish with the rod high. Once that initial run is over, a high stick is very ineffective. Hold the rod to one side, and pull the fish's head toward you rather than lifting it up.

For most anglers, big fish are the main reason for making an Alaskan trip. Finding and fooling them are only part of the adventure. Knowing how to quickly land these big fish and release them without injury will allow you to bring home trophy grip-and-grin photos instead of just stories about the ones that got away.

21

BEARS, BUGS, AND BAD WEATHER

Alaska is different from any other part of the country. It's bigger, wilder, and more unforgiving. For most people, that first step into the unknown can be a bit intimidating. Stories about Alaska's bears, mosquitoes, and legendary storms are part of the state's iconography. And as with most such stories, there is at least a kernel of truth to them. None of these deterrents should keep you from enjoying the superb fishing found here, though. Preparation, attitude, and knowledge will keep everyday problems manageable and extraordinary ones survivable.

BEARS
Let's start with everyone's favorite danger—the state's large population of grizzly bears. If you are fishing in Alaska, sooner or later you will encounter one of them. Salmon are the mainstay of their diet, so anyplace that you find salmon, you will find bears. Don't count on large groups of people to deter the bears from their favorite food. Even within the city limits of Anchorage, you will find trails through the streamside brush that are about three feet high and three feet wide.

The good news is that people are not on the diet. The bears simply want to be left alone to raise their cubs, fatten up on salmon or an unfortunate moose calf, and sleep peacefully in the tall grass. It is when they perceive a person as threatening these activities that there is trouble. With a very few exceptions, bears do not see people as prey. In most cases, a bear's reaction is determined by circumstances, the bear's personality, the distance between you and the bear, and your actions.

Problem Bears

Although all bears are individuals, some types have larger space requirements or are more likely to attack than flee. Most people are concerned about running into a sow with cubs. Interestingly, a black bear sow will bluff and threaten but rarely attack to defend her cubs. Black bears are animals of the woods, and the best protection for the cubs is to send them up a tree and come back for them when the threat is past. Grizzly bears, however, are creatures of the open plains and tundra, and a cub's survival depends on the ferocity with which its mother is prepared to defend it. Grizzly sows with cubs can be very dangerous, but if they become aware of you from a distance, they will always opt to move the cubs away from any perceived risk.

Juvenile bears just out on their own can be very problematic, particularly the young boars. Like teenagers anywhere, they are attempting to find their place and constantly push the limits. They are usually not very good at fishing and may decide that stealing fish from an angler is easier than doing the work themselves. A mature bear may walk into your fishing hole, simply assuming that you will defer to it. Under the same circumstances, a juvenile may challenge you, more interested in determining dominance than in fishing. Most of the problems I've had with bears involved adolescents.

The most impressive of the bears are the big boars. They can be twice the size of the females, ranging from 400 pounds in high tundra to 850 along the salmon streams. The dominant males, their bellies swollen with fish, may weigh more than 1,000 pounds by September. A dispute between two boars sounds like *Jurassic Park* with the volume turned to the max—truly terrifying.

The bears that really frighten me are those guarding a kill. Most bears, including sows with cubs, will get out of your way if they hear you coming. A bear on a kill won't. You need to avoid it. The smell of rotting meat is a bad sign. Look around and then carefully retreat along your approach route. Never investigate a group of ravens or magpies. Moose calving season is the worst time, but hunters' gut piles will also draw bears.

That same food-based territoriality exists in a much-muted form on salmon streams. If a bear has a fishing hole, treat the animal with at least the same respect you would give a fellow angler. I've had bears make it clear that they would not tolerate my wading through their fishing hole, although they had no objection to my walking along the bank at essentially the same distance. I rather share that attitude myself.

The bears I have described may be a problem, but they are just being bears. Without a doubt, the most dangerous bears are those created by people's stupidity: bears that associate people with food. These are the bears that will walk into your camp at night or confront you over that salmon you just beached. And they can be cranky about it. The axiom that a fed bear is a dead bear is glaringly true. They have become too dangerous to tolerate and will almost certainly be shot, hopefully before someone is mauled.

Staying Out of Trouble

Any bear, black or grizzly, can be dangerous if surprised. And in spite of the acuteness of their senses, it's easier to surprise them than you might expect.

Any time you are walking through brush or are in a situation where your view is impeded, it's important to make noise to alert any bears to your presence. This does not mean that you need to sound like Patton's army coming through the woods, driving away every living thing in earshot. And don't wear bear bells, which not only are incredibly annoying to other people, but also don't work with bears. Tom Smith, a federal bear researcher in Alaska, tested the reaction of wild bears to various types of noises. The bears simply ignored the bells, much like they would a birdsong. The two sounds to which all bears immediately alerted were human voices and the sound of a breaking stick.

A simple loud "Hey, bear," repeated at appropriate intervals and intensity, will suffice. Clapping hands is also good, but that's difficult to do when you're carrying a fly rod. On windy days, bears tend to bed down and stay put. Your voice won't carry as far, so be particularly careful if you are walking upwind through high grass or other potential resting areas.

Don't assume that all bears will run just because they become aware of you. If you see a bear, give it the right of way, if for no other reason than you are on the stream just to play. The bear is trying to earn a living.

Pay attention. Look around during your backcast. On several occasions, I've turned around to discover that a bear had quietly slipped well inside my comfort zone, and although the bears in question didn't seem concerned, my cardiologist would have been.

If you're fighting a fish and a bear approaches, break it off. I once ran into a teenage bear that had discovered it was easier to steal fish than to catch them. The sound of a reel screaming was like ringing a dinner bell. Every time someone would hook a fish, the bear would come charging out of the woods at a full gallop. He became known on the river as Psycho Bear. Do not teach a bear this trick.

Don't leave daypacks or other gear lying on the riverbanks. Bears have an intense curiosity born of a large omnivorous appetite, and a pack on a gravel bar will draw their attention every time. They also seem to have a fascination with rubber and similar materials, which include inflatable rafts and folding kayaks. I learned this lesson the hard way when I stashed a pair of waders under an alder while I took a short hike. I returned to find two cubs playing tug-of-war with them, one on each leg.

Never approach a bear, no matter how much you want the photo. They consider it an act of aggression, and it can be poorly received. Long lenses are cheaper than emergency room bills.

There are a few cautions specific to anglers. Bears are most active at night, so late-evening or break-of-dawn fishing can be dicey. Shallow back channels full of spawning salmon are little bear smorgasbords, and you never know who may be sleeping off lunch in the nearby willows. If you keep fish (catch-and-release doesn't necessarily apply to fresh salmon), clean them in the river and pitch the waste into the current. Don't wipe your hands on your waders, and do rinse your net after landing a fish.

Camping on a salmon stream creates a different set of problems. Pitching your tent in the middle of a bear trail is never a good idea, but on many rivers, it's the only option. The primary campsite risk is luring a bear into camp with the prospect of a meal. The basic principle is to avoid anything that would cause a bear to associate people with food. You should minimize food odors, particularly on your clothes or tent, and protect food from scavenging bears. Keep a scrupulously clean camp. This means no dirty dishes, no bags of chips left on the picnic table, no burning garbage in the fire pit. Pick a menu that won't draw bears. Frying bacon or grilling steaks may be all right in a large campground, but I wouldn't do it on a float trip. On extended trips, we cook our meals ahead of time and freeze them, which means we need only to heat them up in a covered pot. I haven't had a problem with food that is stored in a cooler, with each individual item or meal in a separate plastic container, but in some places bears see the coolers as their personal picnic baskets. The bearproof canisters are more effective, and some places require them, although they are heavy, expensive, and of limited space.

Storing food at night is the primary problem. The method you should use is determined by the terrain and the sophistication of the local bears. There are bears in Yosemite that specialize in breaking into specific makes and models of cars. Personally, I'd rather deal with our naive rural bears. If you're in wooded country, you can hang your food in a tree, but remember that black bears can climb. We usually camp on gravel bars surrounded by tundra, so we have no alternative but to leave food on the ground. We place it well away from camp and hope for the best. At night, we move all food, garbage, cooking utensils, and other suspect items a hundred yards from camp and wrap it in a tarp. We leave the food in an open area so that we can see it at all times as we approach it. We also pee on the bear trail so that a bear approaching from upwind is aware of us before it stumbles into the food. It's not a perfect system, and I've occasionally had to chase a curious bear away from the food cache. In thirty years of camping in Alaska, however, I've not yet had a bear get into the food.

The newest form of camp protection is an electric fence. They are now routinely used around research stations, campgrounds, and other permanent establishments and are quite effective in deterring curious bears. A park ranger told me that she watched an adolescent do a full backflip after he touched his nose to the wire. Portable units are also available for about $300. They consist of a roll of wire, a battery and controller, and a solar panel to recharge the battery. An empty camp is a magnet for curious bears, and an electric fence will easily pay for itself if you are fishing from a base camp. But as someone who grew up in cattle country, I find the prospect of getting up in the dark to relieve myself in the proximity of an electric fence almost as frightening as the bears.

Nose to Nose

If you spend enough time on Alaskan rivers, sooner or later you are going to have some personal interaction with a bear. Fortunately, such encounters almost always end peaceably, and acting appropriately will greatly increase your chances of ending up with an amusing campfire tale.

The first option is to get out of the bear's way. If it's walking down the riverbank, either back away from the river or wade across to the other side. Unless you are sure that you can slip away undetected, let the bear know that you are human. Keep your voice calm and talk to him loud enough to be heard. If you're in a group—and in serious bear country, you should be—stand shoulder-to-shoulder. Given adequate room, bears will almost always avoid a confrontation.

A bear that comes into camp huffing and hop-charging you is trying to drive you away from your food. Make noise, bang on pans, and attempt to drive it away. Noisily flapping a raincoat at a bear can be surprisingly effective. If it's a black bear, throw rocks at it, like you would a mean dog. Be careful about hitting a grizzly bear with a rock, though—it just pisses them off. Rocks thrown into the water near a bear can be effective, and I've seen experienced guides use their hands to splash water toward bears that were overly curious.

If you stumble into a bear or one assertively approaches you, you need to convince him that he should not try messing with you. *Do not run.* You want to convey the idea that you are not looking for trouble but are willing and able to defend yourself if attacked. Follow the example of other bears that are faced with your situation: Stand your ground. Some experts recommend that you avoid eye contact with a bear. Look at the ground next to the animal and watch it from the corner of your eyes. Talk to it calmly and quietly. Yawning, turning sideways, salivating, or frothing at the mouth are signs of stress in a bear but are not necessarily precursors to a charge.

Depending on the distance, you may be able to back up slowly or move to one side and let the bear pass. If it's too close, though, you may not be able to withdraw without risking an attack. In a confrontation between two bears, the dominant animal gets to decide when to walk away. Under those circumstances, let the bear make that decision.

Standing your ground with an aggressive bear is an unpleasant experience. It's even harder if the bear decides to charge. Nevertheless, that's exactly what you must do. Fortunately, most charges are bluffs, and if you do not run, the bear will veer off before contact. And if it doesn't veer off? Well, that's the next subject.

Surviving a Bear Attack

I am happy to say that neither I nor anyone I know have any personal anecdotes about being attacked by a bear. Very few people do.

Defending yourself is the first option, which means either a gun or pepper spray. Don't even consider a gun unless you're sufficiently familiar with it to get a shell in the chamber, the safety off, and aim it at a moving target, all without a conscious thought. It takes a heavy slug to stop a bear. A shotgun with rifled slugs or a .30-06 caliber rifle with a 220-grain bullet is the minimum. The gun of choice for most professionals who are in regular contact with bears is a marine-finished short-barrel shotgun. If you do have to shoot a bear, be aware that a brain shot is very difficult; a heart-lung shot will kill it but may not knock it down immediately; and a bear cannot run with a broken shoulder. With a head-on charging bear, aim just below the chin. And if your trigger finger gets twitchy, keep in mind that even if the trooper's investigation of the killing determines that it was justified, you will need to skin the bear, salvage the hide, and turn it in to the state, or you will be prosecuted for wanton waste of a game animal. And no, you can't keep so much as a single claw.

Some people like to carry a heavy-caliber pistol, but unless you can hit a charging animal in a very precise spot, you are going to have a very angry bear to deal with. Even a .44 magnum has less than half the stopping power of the '06 that I mentioned as a minimum gun. Pepper spray, made from hot peppers, may not provide the macho swagger you get from packing a big pistol, but it gives you—and the bear—a much better chance of escaping an attack unharmed. It is an effective deterrent. Just imagine rubbing a habañero pepper in your eyes. In almost every instance, it's a better option than a handgun.

If you are actually attacked, your life may depend on the correct response, and that is determined in part by the species of bear with which you are dealing. A grizzly attack is usually in response to a perceived threat, and once that threat is neutralized, the bear will break off the attack. Lie facedown, with your hands locked behind your neck and legs spread slightly so the bear can't easily flip you over. Don't move until you're sure the bear has left the area. A second attack may occur if you move, and it's likely to be more vicious than the first.

There are extremely rare exceptions to the people-are-not-prey rule, usually involving black bears and occurring in remote areas where the bears are not accustomed to people. If you are attacked by a black bear, do not play dead unless you're certain it's a mother defending her cubs. Fight back with anything you can find—knives, rocks, clubs.

People have also been killed by predatory grizzlies in a few recent incidents, so there are exceptions to all rules about bears. A predatory bear will not make threat displays but may try to circle you. Never let a bear get behind you. If you believe that a bear is stalking you, even if it appears only curious, try a show of aggression, such as splashing water at it or throwing rocks toward it, although it's usually best not to plunk it.

There's a special adrenaline-based pleasure to being in country with bears, particularly grizzly bears. The risk of trouble is very slight, but you feel a sense of wildness that is not present on domesticated rivers.

BUGS

The bears get all the press, but the bugs are far more bloodthirsty. Mosquitoes are the most notorious but not necessarily the worst. Alaska also has a myriad of biting flies and gnats, as well as healthy populations of yellow jackets. Fortunately, insect repellents with a high DEET content do a good job of keeping most of them at bay.

Mosquitoes are at their worst in the early part of the season, and you can encounter clouds of them on some tundra rivers. DEET is almost completely effective against them, but it spells death for fly-line finishes and some plastics, so be judicious in its application. Sticks of repellent avoid the problem of overspray, but the mosquitoes will find every gap in your application. I like the little pump bottles. Apply it only to the backs of your hands. Mosquito coils are good at keeping the numbers under control around camp.

Biting flies come in a variety of sizes. The most annoying are white socks, a tiny blackfly that bites only rarely—at least compared with mosquitoes. DEET will keep them from biting, but not from tormenting you by crawling on the inside of your glasses or up your nose, usually when you have both hands occupied with a big fish.

Some areas have deerflies and horseflies that take a chunk of meat when they bite you. There are also blackflies similar to those of the Maine woods; they're slow but have painful bites. They are usually a problem in the woods rather than on the stream, however, so they are of less consequence to fishers than hikers. A small orangish red fly, which family newspapers euphemistically refer to as "a little red fellow," is my personal nemesis. It will crawl along your clothing until it finds DEET-free flesh along your hat brim or the top of your socks. Its bites cause a reaction in some people and typically take weeks to heal.

Biting gnats, called no-see-ums, are common during August, usually at night. A hole in the mosquito netting of your tent is an invitation to a night of scratching and slapping at unseen annoyances.

Hot summers usually mean a lot of yellow jackets. They tend to be in brushy areas, so listen for the telltale hum of an angry hive. The stings are painful but not serious unless you're allergic to them. If you are, carry a sting kit if you plan to fish in wooded or brushy areas.

You can do three things to minimize the annoyance of the various bugs. The first is to avoid them. Camp on gravel bars where there is no cover and a bit of a breeze. Tundra camps can be really bad, but rural villages seem to be the worst. The mosquitoes are a lot less of a problem when you're out on the river than when you're in camp. Mosquitoes are much thicker in June than during August, and they're just about nonexistent after the first frost.

The second thing is use protection. Long sleeves, a hat, and DEET will keep most bugs from biting. If they are truly bad, a head net will give complete relief, but these are not very comfortable, and you see few Alaskans wearing them. Mosquito coils do a good job of cutting down the numbers in camp. When space limitations allow, we take a large tent with walls of netting to use for cooking and eating.

The third and most important tactic is to learn to ignore them—easier said than done. Most people quickly develop a type of immunity to mosquito bites. After a few days, the bites will itch for a few minutes and then essentially disappear. Although insect repellent keeps mosquitoes and other bugs from biting, they will still hover around you, looking for a breach in the chemical armor. At this point, though, the impact is pretty much psychological. White socks and blackflies are more annoying and in short order can drive a person to wearing a head net.

You can't escape completely from the bugs in Alaska, but you can minimize their impact enough that they won't prevent you from having fun. And if they get too bad, just think what it was like for the people who lived here before DEET and mosquito netting.

BAD WEATHER

Of the three major drawbacks to fishing in Alaska, weather is the most likely to detract from your trip. It's also the most dangerous. Like the bears and the bugs, though, problems can be minimized with a bit of foresight and preparation.

Most of the fishing in Alaska takes place within a hundred miles of the coast, meaning that you are at the mercy of marine weather systems, typically cool and wet. June and July are usually benign, with frequent sunny days and temperatures that can reach the seventies. Fog and rain can occur at any time, however, and it's not unusual for the weather to go from hot and sunny to cold, wet, and windy in a few hours.

August and September are the prime fishing months for trout and coho, but they are also the worst months for weather. August usually brings a change in the predominant weather systems, with frequent rain and the occasional serious storm. September can be very rainy, with frosty nights.

The commercial fishers have a saying, though: "There is no such thing as bad weather, just bad gear." Good gear is the key to ensuring that you stay warm and dry, whether you're fishing a roadside stream next to your RV or spending a weeklong float trip camping on gravel bars. People from arid climates frequently don't realize that once you get wet here, you won't dry out. You simply cannot count on the sun coming out and making everything okay.

High-quality raingear is essential. The best raincoats for fishing are the short-cut Gore-Tex wading jackets made by several top-quality manufacturers. They come in two weights. The lightweight jacket is adequate for everything but late-season fishing or extended camping

trips where you may be in driving rain for several days. If you are camping, a pair of Gore-Tex pants will keep your legs dry and allow you to
sit on wet surfaces. If you're on a tight budget, the rubberized Helly
Hansen–type gear used by commercial fishermen will keep the rain
out, although it won't breathe and isn't particularly comfortable. Don't
even consider trying to get by with the light plastic or nylon jackets
designed for golfers and gardeners. Most important, never leave camp
without your raingear, and put it on before you get wet.

Clothing should be layered. Although it's necessary to prepare for
bad weather, that doesn't mean you won't spend a lot of time in warm
sunshine. I like long-sleeved cotton shirts for good days. They keep the
bugs off and are not too hot. A lightweight poly undershirt or a vest in
the daypack will provide enough warmth if the weather cools. On cold
days, nothing beats pile. It's light and stays warm when it's wet. Carry a
lightweight stocking cap and a pair of poly liner gloves, particularly if
you're doing a run in a boat.

If you're camping, particularly on long float trips, you need bullet-
proof protection from driving rain. That means a good three-season
tent with a full rain fly. You also need a tarp to set up as shelter for
cooking and eating. Your system for holding the tarp up must be able
to handle a lot of wind. It won't do you any good if you can't hold it
in place. Make the effort necessary to keep your clothes, sleeping bag,
and tent floor dry.

Summer weather in Alaska can be less than ideal at times, but good
equipment makes it easily manageable. Bad equipment and bad judgment, though, can make it dangerous. People die from exposure or
hypothermia because they wander out into the woods in a cotton
T-shirt and get lost. Others drown trying to wade or float rivers that
are at flood stage. Still others are obsessed with getting back to the
office on time and fly in marginal weather. All of these tragedies are
avoidable. With a little common sense and patience, the worst that will
happen is a few hours of discomfort.

The occasional hardship or adrenaline surge is part of fishing in
Alaska. There may be times when you really wish you were somewhere
else. But you can take comfort in the thought that if it weren't for the
bears, bugs, and bad weather, this place would be just like Los Angeles.

22

THE
FLY BOX

Look in any fly catalog and you'll find the "Alaskan Selection." It invariably includes egg patterns, flesh flies, Egg-Sucking Leeches, and Deerhair Mice. There usually is a salmon variation with a variety of brightly colored leeches, Krystal-bodied Buggers, and Flash Flies. Every guide's fly box includes his or her preferred version of all these flies. Most guides also have their own personal favorites that aren't easily found in the fly shops. And in addition to these specialty flies, there is a place for some traditional patterns—you just have to know which ones are most effective. Given the broad universe of Alaskan flies, the question is which ones you need for a particular trip.

Like everything about Alaskan fishing, fly selection is a matter of timing. Trout in June are not looking for eggs, and don't expect to catch September fish on a fry pattern. Dry flies can be effective during early summer, but few trout will be looking up once the salmon start to spawn. Knowing which flies are effective for different species and at different times of the year will save you money at the fly shop or time at the vise.

TROUT PATTERNS
It is perhaps too obvious to mention, but the key to selecting the right fly for trout, Dolly Varden, and grayling is to imitate what they are eating. Obvious, but too often ignored. The starting point in identifying the trout food du jour is the salmon spawning cycle.

Salmon eggs hatch in late spring, and the tiny alevins, their yolk sacs still attached, wriggle out of the gravel. By the time the season opens, they have absorbed the yolk sacs and are free-swimming fry. Patterns that imitate these baby salmon are the early-season standard on most rivers. Fry are about an inch long, swim with a full-body motion, and have large, prominent eyes. The best flies match these characteristics. The fry that have been hiding back in the flooded grass will be dark and mottled, but those that have been along the rocky edges tend to be more silver.

There are several hard-bodied fry patterns that look remarkably like a dead fry. They can be effective fished along the bottom like a nymph. Flies with a bit more inherent movement can also be fished deep under an indicator and are usually more effective. Fry typically migrate in the upper water column and the trout will hit imitations fished right in the film. Any small streamer, size 10 or 12, with brown or olive over white and a little flash will work, but the most consistent producer is a very sparsely tied Thunder Creek. This fly is normally made with bucktail, but try tying some with softer fibers like marabou, Craft Fur, or arctic fox.

Sockeye spawning streams are not the only place to fish in the early season. Depending on the river, king, chum, pink, or coho fry may be present. Pink and chum fry migrate directly to the sea, and you can fish fry patterns in the estuaries for Dollies and cutthroat. Kings and cohos spend several years in fresh water and, like the year-old sockeye fry, go to sea as smolt. Smolt are usually about two and a half to three inches long. Smolt patterns are deadly on any river that drains a sockeye lake or has a run of king salmon. Like most lake-dwelling fish, sockeye smolt are primarily silver, with some dark coloration on the back. There are a few specific smolt patterns, but they are often tied too small. I like Double Bunnies, white Bunny Leeches, white Krystal Buggers, and Clousers. Muddler Minnows can also be good. Because smolt tend to migrate near the surface, and a lot of fish are injured by the constant attack of trout, gulls, and terns, topwater patterns like Crease Flies and small sliders can sometimes be a lot of fun.

Early-season trout are very opportunistic, and the most consistent patterns are often big, dark flies worked right on the bottom in front of their noses. Sculpins, leeches, and lamprey larvae are prevalent in almost all of the rivers, and big trout like a big meal. Wooly Buggers, Bunny Flies, and Sculpin patterns are mandatory, and I carry them in black, olive, and purple. They should be weighted or tied with coneheads or lead eyes. String Leeches and Articulated Leeches, some as long as three inches, are deadly.

Alaska is not known for its dry-fly fishing, but under the right conditions, it can be spectacular. Warm, sunny days from June through mid-July often produce enough caddis, midges, and mayflies to get a few noses up. Some rivers even get hatches of big green drakes or large black stoneflies. You won't see the steady, rhythmic feeding that occurs on classic trout streams, but any time you see fish rising sporadically, you stand a good chance of fooling them. Flies are pretty straightforward. In addition to a couple of big attractors, like Stimulators or a Madam X, I carry Parachute Adams, Elk Hair Caddis, and Black Gnats. Emerger patterns are good, and although the fish are occasionally selective to tiny ones, most of the time a size 14 will work.

The quintessential Alaskan dry fly is the Deerhair Mouse. Tundra streams, particularly those in the southwestern part of the state, have huge populations of voles and other small rodents. When one of them ends up in the water, it is a meal that big trout and char can't pass up. The cute little Deerhair Mice with ears and whiskers may catch fly fishers, but they are poor candidates for the fly box. They usually have realistically down-sloping faces, so when they are skated, they tend to dive. In addition, although deer hair makes a wonderful fly, it tends to become waterlogged and won't float quite high enough for the best action. The secret is a foam back, which not only provides additional buoyancy, but also presents a planing surface that will keep the fly skating perfectly. My favorite is the Morrish Mouse, but other, similar patterns work equally well.

Nymphs are far more effective than many people realize, and they are an early-season standard for many experienced Alaskan fly fishers. They continue to fish well throughout the summer, though, and some of the best nymph fishing occurs as the female salmon are digging their redds. The trout are already holding below them, waiting for the eggs to fall. Instead, they get a steady smorgasbord of nymphs dislodged by the redd building. Even after the salmon begin to spawn, you can often get a stubborn rainbow to take a well-drifted nymph. I carry Flashback

Pheasant Tails, Hare's Ears, and Prince Nymphs in sizes 12 to 16 and probably 90 percent of time use a beadhead.

For many anglers, Alaska means fishing egg patterns, and during August it can be difficult to interest trout in anything else. They are laying in the fat they need to survive the winter and are single-mindedly eating as many eggs as their bodies can process. Beads are popular as an egg pattern, but there are alternatives for those who believe that using a fly is an essential part of fly fishing. Glo-Bugs are still the fly of choice, and Chuck Ash's version is particularly effective. Other egg patterns incorporate beads and other materials onto the hook, but they are hard and the trout spit them out immediately. Some of the softer plastics get around that problem.

Whatever you choose, size and color are critical. King salmon eggs are larger, about ten millimeters in diameter, and have more orange in them than sockeye eggs, which are about six to eight millimeters. The color of the eggs changes as they spend time in the water, ranging from the classic orangish pink to a flat cream yellow. As the season progresses, the fish see more variety, and the color of choice may change from day to day. If you are getting refusals, your problem is probably your drift, the size of the fly, or the color—in that order.

Most of the guides in Alaska now use beads as egg imitations. Even those who would prefer to use traditional flies have been forced by the competition to switch—and there is no question that beads are remarkably effective. Much of their effectiveness, and most of the controversy, comes from the way they are rigged. The bead is slid onto the leader and typically pegged, held in place with a broken-off toothpick above a bare hook. A fish that picks up the bead cannot spit it out without the leader dragging through its mouth and hooking it, typically on the outside of mandible. If the distance between the bead and hook is too great, the fish ends up with the hook in its eye or gills. In order to prevent these injuries, state regulations now prohibit pegging more than two inches above the hook.

Pegging beads has made a huge difference in the success rates on big, turbulent rivers like the Kenai. Getting a dead drift on the bottom and detecting very soft takes are mutually exclusive on rivers like that. On smaller streams, pegging is not really necessary, although it covers a lot of mistakes in detecting subtle strikes.

Most Alaskan fly shops now carry a selection of beads in various sizes and colors. Most guides carry a variety of colors and paint the beads with pearlescent nail polish. The late Curt Trout was a master at imitating the eggs found on the Kenai and took great delight in challenging a fly-shop customer to spot the fakes in a handful of eggs and beads. If you are trying to match beads with the natural eggs in the stream, do it underwater, where you can get an accurate comparison.

If you decide to use beads, check the regulations first. Beads do not meet the state's definition of a fly and are classified as attractors. They are now illegal in fly-fishing-only waters in south-central Alaska, although not in other areas of the state. You may not use a bare hook below the bead in any fly-fishing-only water. Most guides opt for a simple, rudimentary fly in those areas.

The final type of Alaskan flies, from a seasonal standpoint, is flesh flies. For tiers who spend their winters crafting exquisite Catskill-type drys, these are the ultimate disillusionment, surpassing even egg patterns. Not only are they a reminder that a fish we have endowed with nobility relishes carrion, but the flies themselves are nothing more than some marabou or bunny fur lashed to a hook. The fact remains, though, that trout and char living in salmon streams make it through the winter on the nutrition provided by the carcasses.

The most common flesh flies are a mixture of dirty white and a bit of salmon pink. Tie one as a Conehead String Leech, with a bit of flash, and you have a pattern that will pull big trout from deep water. The big Bunny Leeches aren't always as effective as a smaller fly. There is so much food in the water at this time of year that fish will sometimes pass up a big chunk of flesh in favor of a tidbit. When that happens, I like roughly dubbed marabou, in the same colors, on a size 8 through 12 hook. Early in the year, if you are fishing on a river, like the Kenai, that sees a large salmon harvest—with scraps of filleted salmon thrown back in the river—try a bright reddish orange fly. Trout will stack up below the cleaning stations and gorge on the leftovers.

As long as we are on the subject of disgusting flies, don't forget a few maggot patterns. They are particularly effective after a fall rain has washed the fly-blown carcasses into the river. These are even easier to tie than flesh flies. Simply wrap some dirty white poly yarn around the shank of a size 12 or 14 scud hook.

By late season, when the eggs are gone and the carcasses have washed downstream, leeches and sculpins can once again be added to your fly box. The fish are fat and still trying to put on as much weight as possible, so big meals are the order of the day. Colder water temperatures will put the fish on the bottom, so put some weight in the flies.

KING SALMON PATTERNS

Kings, like all salmon, quit feeding once they enter fresh water, which means that there are two different sets of flies to consider. For those few anglers who go after kings in the salt, the flies should be realistic depictions of their prey species, principally herring, sand lance, smelt, eulachon, and similar small baitfish. Adding the irregular action of a wounded fish helps trigger strikes, so the most effective flies are often patterns like Clousers or the various epoxy-headed flies, which will twitch and dive on the retrieve. Sea Habits, Deceivers, and the Clouser Half-and-Halfs are all good patterns.

Most fly fishing for kings takes place in fresh water, and these flies are at the other end of the spectrum. Far from realistic, they tend to be big, garish, and flashy. Kings like the deepest parts of the rivers, and they will rarely move up to take a fly. You need a fly that will go to the bottom. In most cases, the fly is not stripped but relies on its materials to give it life. Finally, kings are very fickle, and the colors that worked yesterday, or a half hour ago, may be ignored on the next cast. Carry a variety of colors and styles, and be prepared to change flies often if the fish are not cooperative.

Flies should be large, usually tied on 1/0 and 2/0 hooks. Marabou and bunny fur provide a pulsating action to the fly without the need to strip it. Colors should generally be bright, although black alone or with other colors can also be effective. Fuchsia, hot pink, orange, red, chartreuse, and yellow are all good colors, and combinations of them are even better. Tinsel and Flashabou add to the allure. The patterns themselves are less important than the characteristics, but Popsicles, Super Prawns, Marabou Speys, Fat Freddies, and big String Leeches all incorporate the important aspects of good chinook flies. Chinook that have reached the upper stretches of the rivers will also hit single-egg patterns, which can come as a surprise when you are fishing for trout.

COHO FLIES

Coho flies fall into three categories: saltwater, conventional freshwater, and topwater patterns. Saltwater patterns are similar to those used for saltwater Chinook—tied to imitate the forage fish on which the salmon prey. Herring, smelt, and sand lance are the most common prey species, and the flies should imitate them in size, color, and flash. Sea Habits, Hareball Leeches, and Popovics's epoxy-headed flies not only imitate the shape and color of the baitfish, but also have an action that resembles a small fish in distress. One of the most effective patterns is the Clouser Minnow, and not surprisingly, the color of choice is chartreuse and white. The Surf Candies and anchovy patterns developed for East Coast stripers and blues do a good job of imitating the thin profile of the sand lance, which is a favorite food of coho staging in the estuaries and river mouths.

The fly patterns for freshwater coho are dramatically different from the realistic baitfish patterns used in the salt. They are bright and flashy, designed to trigger an aggressive response rather than hunger. Chartreuse, hot pink, orange, purple, and fuchsia are all good colors, and combinations of them, particularly with a little black added, can be even better. Flashabou, Krystal Flash, and Krystal Chenille all add to their effectiveness, and some patterns, like the Karluk Flash Fly, are primarily tinsel.

In the slow backwaters that draw resting silvers, the best flies are those that move and pulsate on their own between twitches. Marabou, bunny fur, and arctic fox are the materials of choice. In faster water, Woolly Buggers may have more life, and a lot of silvers have fallen to Egg-Sucking Leeches and chartreuse and black Buggers. George Davis's Spankers, which are little more than a ball of fluorescent Krystal Flash, can also be deadly. Silvers generally like a fly that is moving, so choose your materials to match the current.

Undoubtedly, skating big flies on the surface has become the most exciting way to catch cohos. The earliest effective patterns were Pink Pollywogs in some variation. They suffered from the same problems as all deer-hair surface patterns: They get waterlogged, they are miserable to cast, they are hard to tie, and they aren't very durable, particularly when they are getting chewed on by big buck cohos. Today there are a number of effective alternatives, mostly tied with a foam back. Hot Lips, Coho Seizures, and Gurglers are all good. Most are still tied in hot pink.

SOCKEYE FLIES

Unlike their piscivorous cousins, sockeyes in the salt feed on euphausi-ids and krill, tiny organisms that make catching them on a rod and reel almost impossible. A few saltwater anglers have had some success sight-fishing to concentrated schools of fish by using the small shrimp pat-terns usually reserved for bonefish. Tied in pink, green, or red and fished on a floating line, these flies will occasionally be picked up by cruising fish. Takes are very subtle. A few kayakers pick up the occa-sional salmon dinner by trolling very sparse shrimp patterns as they cruise the shorelines of Southeast or Prince William Sound. Crazy Charlies, Teeny Nymphs, and similar flies will work, but the most effec-tive may be a fly called the Red Hot. It consists of nothing but a red Gamakatsu hook dressed with a few strands of red Flashabou.

Sockeyes in fresh water are notoriously reluctant to hit a fly. They rarely will actively chase a fly the way that cohos or chinook will. Many anglers believe that the sockeye's ocean diet means that it lacks the search image that triggers strikes in other species of salmon. Whatever the reason, the flies used for sockeyes are far different from those tied for the other species. The most effective flies are sparse and small, sizes 4 to 8. Montana Brassies, Comets, Sockeye Johns, and Sockeye Specials all work well. The Red Hot described above is good, as is a variation tied with a wisp of apple green yarn instead of the Flashabou.

STEELHEAD FLIES

Fly tiers love steelhead patterns—the West Coast equivalent of Atlantic salmon flies. They encompass everything from bright fluorescent colors to small, elegant low-water patterns to large, black String Leeches—and they all work. Rather, I should say they all work sometimes. An experienced steelheader will carry a range of patterns that includes flies appropriate for all conditions. That essentially means a selection of both bright and dark flies, ranging from small (size 8) and sparsely tied to very large (the aforementioned String Leech). In addition, most Alaskans carry a variety of Glo-Bugs, in a range of colors and sizes.

Steelhead are fished with two different techniques, and those techniques determine the type of fly. A classic downstream swing, usually on a sinking-tip line, works best with a traditional streamer type of pattern. The steelhead flies popularized in the Northwest, such as Skunks, Freight Trains, Signal Lights, and Comets, work well, but most Alaskan steelheaders prefer flies with more inherent action. These include Bunny Leeches, Marabou Speys, and Super Prawns. Woolly Buggers and Egg-Sucking Leeches are also good. For larger rivers or high water, a big String Leech, usually tied in black or purple, is often the first choice.

Most fly fishers look first to bright patterns for steelhead. Hot pink, red, fuchsia, and orange are the usual colors, but it is always good to have a couple of chartreuse or bright green alternatives. Dark flies are best in black and purple, often with a red or green accent. For low-water conditions, flies that are tied sparse and with more subdued colors work best.

Many of the state's smaller streams are best fished with a floating line and strike indicator. It may not be traditional, but upstream casts and tight lies make a sinking tip impossible at times. Glo-Bugs are the usual fly of choice for fishing with an indicator, although not necessarily as egg imitations—they may be three-quarters of an inch in diameter and a mixture of chartreuse, fuchsia, and black. There are other flies that work equally well. Marabou Speys or a simple palmered hackle will provide a broad silhouette on a dead drift and have more inherent life than a Glo-Bug. A couple wraps of cerise bunny fur around a size 6 hook makes a great pattern for dead drifting under an indicator. The steelhead nymphs used in the Great Lakes fisheries have not caught on in Alaska, but there are occasions, usually in low, clear water, where a drab nymph pattern will fool spooky fish.

AT THE VISE

The flies that I have discussed here are generally available from the fly shops. But every guide has a few favorites, and they are not always found in the catalogs or pattern books. Below are the tying recipes for some of the less common patterns that are mentioned in the guide interviews. I have also included instructions on tying the sometimes confusing String Leeches and Articulated Leeches.

BUNNY LEECH

The Bunny Leech is a standard for almost every species. Size and color vary.

Hook:	Size 6–3/0.
Weight:	Lead wire or weighted eyes (optional).
Thread:	3/0 to match body or create contrasting head.
Tail:	Zonker strip.
Body:	Crosscut rabbit palmered over entire body.
Wing:	Few strands of Flashabou along each side (optional).

ARTICULATED LEECH

This is a tying style, rather than a specific pattern. Articulated Leeches are standard for many species. They are typically about 3 inches long. Colors vary, but black is the most useful for trout.

Hook:	Size 4–2/0, front hook cut at bend, rear hook straight-eye salmon hook.
Thread:	3/0 color to match fly.
Joint:	30-pound Dacron; the joint should be short enough to be hidden by the rabbit fur extending from the front hook.
Tail:	Zonker strip with a few strands of Flashabou.
Rear body:	Crosscut rabbit strip.
Front body:	Crosscut rabbit strip.
Eyes:	Stainless deep-water, bead-chain, or dazzle eyes; conehead may be substituted.

HAREBALL LEECH (ARTICULATED LEECH)

Hook:	Size 4–2/0, front hook cut at bend, rear hook straight-eye salmon hook.
Thread:	White 3/0.
Joint:	30-pound Dacron.
Tail:	White Zonker strip, purple and pearl Flashabou.
Rear body:	White Krystal Chenille ribbed with white crosscut rabbit strip.
Front body:	White Krystal Chenille ribbed with white crosscut rabbit strip.
Eyes:	Stainless deep-water eyes.

STRING LEECH

The String Leech is a tying style, rather than a specific pattern. Like the Articulated Leech, it incorporates two hooks, with the bend and point cut off the front hook. The difference is that the connection between the two hooks is longer, and the body material, usually a rabbit Zonker strip, is brought forward from the rear hook to the front hook. The result is a fly that can be much longer than an Articulated Leech.

Hook:	Size 4–2/0, front hook cut at bend, rear hook straight-eye salmon hook.
Thread:	3/0 color to match fly.
Joint:	30-pound Dacron or braided nylon for total length of 3 to 5 inches.
Tail:	Zonker strip with a few strands of Flashabou.
Body:	Zonker strip (continue the tail) tied in at bend and behind eye of rear hook; strip is brought forward to front hook and tied in at bend and behind eye to create a single long body.
Underbody:	Krystal Chenille (optional).
Eyes:	Stainless deep-water, bead-chain, or dazzle eyes; conehead may be substituted.

STARLIGHT LEECH

The Starlight Leech can be made in black, pink, purple, or various color combinations: red head with black tail and body; orange and black; chartreuse and black; or red and white.

Hook:	Size 2–4, 2X long-shank salmon up-eye hook.
Thread:	Black.
Tail:	Zonker strip.
Body:	Large Ice or Cactus Chenille.
Hackle:	Collar of saddle hackle to match body.
Head:	Chenille or Krystal Chenille wrapped around eyes.
Eyes:	Stainless deep–water eyes.

DAVIS SPANKER

Hook:	Size 2, heavy salmon up-eye hook.
Thread:	3/0 to match body.
Tail:	Pearl Flashabou, about 30 strands, 1 1/2 times the body length.
Body:	Ice or Cactus Chenille, hot pink or chartreuse.
Wing:	Pearl Krystal Flash slightly longer than body.
Head:	Pearl or hot pink Ice or Cactus Chenille.

SPARKLE SHRIMP

Hook:	Size 2–6 heavy salmon up-eye hook.
Thread:	3/0 to match body.
Body:	Krystal Chenille, fuchsia or chartreuse.
Hackle:	Palmered saddle hackle to match body.
Tail and shell:	Pearl Flashabou, tied as tail and continued over the body as a shell.

BRASSIE (SOCKEYE)

Hook:	Size 2–4 heavy salmon up-eye hook.
Thread:	3/0 black.
Body:	Brass wire.
Wing:	Short, sparse white calf tail or substitute.

SOCKEYE ORANGE OR GREEN

Hook:	Size 2–6 heavy nymph hook.
Thread:	3/0 black.
Body:	Small dubbed ball of gold Krystal Dub just behind wing.
Throat:	Orange or green saddle hackle.
Wing:	Short, sparse black calf tail or substitute.

HOT LIPS

Hook:	Size 4 wide-gap hook.
Thread:	3/0 pink.
Tail:	White and hot pink marabou, topped with a few strands of blue Flashabou.
Underbody:	Hot pink 2-millimeter foam, the front end extending ¼ inch past the hook eye and rounded to create bottom "lip."
Body:	Hot pink Ice or Cactus Chenille.
Back:	Hot pink 2-millimeter foam, the front end extending ¼ inch past the hook eye to form the upper "lip," rear end extending ¼ inch past the tie-in point.

JACK HOLMAN'S FRY FLY

Hook:	Size 10 short-shank hook.
Thread:	6/0 white.
Overwing:	Pearl Krystal Flash tied facing forward at eye of hook.
Head:	White or pearl bead pulled over Krystal Flash tie-in point.
Thread:	3/0 red.
Wing:	White Polar Fiber Hair, Craft Fur, or substitute tied directly behind bead.
Overwing:	Pull Krystal Flash back over bead and temporarily secure at bend of hook; coat head with epoxy and let set before releasing Krystal Flash.
Eyes:	Black pupils painted over bead.

MAGGOT FLY

Hook:	Size 12–14 scud hook.
Thread:	3/0 white.
Body:	White latex, poly yarn, or floss.

BILLY'S KRYSTAL EGG

Hook:	Size 10–12 egg hook.
Bead:	1/8-inch gold tungsten bead.
Tail:	Four strands pink pearlescent Krystal Flash, short.
Body:	Iliamna pink McFly Foam, tied as Glo-Bug.

Index

Afognak Island, 100, 105
Akwe River, 127
Alaganik Slough, 128
Alagnak River, 19, 24–26, 28, 29
Alevins, 4–5
ALFs, 118, 132
American Creek, 3, 4, 10
American River, 99
Aniak River, 36, 37, 40–41
A.P. Nymph, 48
Articulated Leech, 10, 13, 28,
    30–31, 79, 105, 117, 132, 167,
    174, 175
Ash, Chuck, 2, 42–53, 168
Ayakulik River, 99, 101, 102, 105

Battle Creeks, 93, 143
Bear Creek, 105
Bears, 5–6, 14, 31, 97–98, 154–161
Beads, pegged, 7, 13, 29–30, 58,
    64, 67, 106, 168–169
  color of, 67
  opposition to using, 45–46
  size of, 67
Billy's Krystal Egg, 46, 178
Bird's Nests, 12
Boga Grip, 135
Branch River Air, 27
Brassies, 50, 177
Bugmeisters, 11

Bunny Flies, 10, 50, 51, 69, 78, 91,
    167
Bunny Leech, 132, 144, 166, 174
Busch, Dan, 95, 104–110
Buskin River, 99, 107

Caddis, 11
  patterns, 44, 48
Char, 7, 62
Chinooks, 102
Chums, 33–34, 37, 51
Circle hooks, 68
Clear Creek, 84, 89
Clothing, 14–15, 163–164
Clouser Minnows, 142, 145
Clousers, 116, 117, 132, 166, 170
Cohos (silvers), 20, 34–35, 37,
    48–49, 85, 91–92
  flies, 60, 171–172
  on the Kenai River, 62, 78–79
  Kodiak, 100–101, 107–109
  in salt water, 112–113, 116–117
  in the Southeast, 138–139,
    143–144
  on the surface, 129–135
Coho Seizure, 132
Cooper Johns, 12
Coulliette, Billy, 55, 73–80
Crazy Charlies, 50, 172
Crease Flies, 117, 166

Dahlberg Diver, 132
Dahlberg Slider, 131–132
Davis, George, 95, 123, 127, 128, 129–135
Davis Spanker, 132, 135, 171, 176
Dead drift fishing, 106
Deceivers, 132, 170
Deerhair Mouse, 44–45, 167
Denali Angler's Lodge, 87
Deshka River, 83, 84–85
Doame River, 127
Dog Salmon, 101
Dollies, 38, 47, 58, 92, 102–103, 139, 141–146
Dry flies, 11
  skated, 106–107, 123, 127, 129–135

East Alsek River, 127
Egg-Sucking Leech, 10, 44, 47, 48, 50, 51, 91, 105, 132
Elk Hair Caddis, 11
Eyak River, 128

Fat Freddie, 50, 90
Flashabou, 79, 132
Flashback Pheasant Tails, 12, 167–168
Flash Flies, 90, 132
Flashtail Minnows, 117
Flesh flies, 31, 69–70, 169
Floating line, 15
Float trips, 51–53
Float tubes, 108
Fluorocarbon, 31–32, 50
Fly-out lodges, selecting, 15–17
Fly patterns, 46–47, 165–177

Gear, selection of, 14–15, 31, 164
Gerken, Ted, 8

Glo-Bugs, 30, 64, 78, 106, 143, 145, 168
Gold Comets, 50
Gold-Ribbed Hare's Ear, 70
Goll, Chris, 8
Goodnews River, 36, 37, 41
Graham, Keith, 96, 114, 115–121
Grayling, 47–48
Green Drake, 11

Hareball Leech, 117, 175
Hare's Ears, 64, 168
Holman, Jack, 1, 8–17
  Fry Fly, 178
Holman, John and Matt, 9
Hooks, 132
Hot Lips, 132, 177

Icy Bay, 128, 129
Iliamna Lake, 22
Iliamna Pinkies, 30
Insects, 161–163
Italio River, 126–127

Kaliakh River, 128
Kanektok River, 36, 37, 39–40
Karluk Flash Fly, 132
Karluk River, 99, 101, 102, 104–105
Katmai Adventures, 27
Kenai Lake, 58, 59
Kenai Fjords, 112
  National Park, 116
Kenai National Wildlife Refuge, 60–61, 71
Kenai River, 55, 57–65
  salmon fishing on, 73–80
  trout fishing on, 66–72
Kiklukh River, 128

Kings, 32–33, 37, 49–50, 58,
    62–63, 84, 89–90, 113,
    144–145
  patterns, 170
Kodiak Island, 97–103
  fly-fishing, 104–110
Krystal Buggers, 166
Kvichak River, 5, 19, 22–24, 28,
    29

Lake Creek, 83, 84–85
Landing techniques, 149–153
Leaders, 15, 32, 76, 107, 131
Leeches
  Articulated, 10, 13, 28, 30–31,
    79, 105, 132, 167, 174
  Articulated Hareball, 117, 175
  Bunny, 132, 144, 166, 174
  Egg-Sucking, 10, 44, 47, 48, 50,
    51, 91, 105, 132
  Starlight, 176
  String, 28, 167, 175
Leopard bows, 37, 44
Litnik River, 100, 105
Little Susitna River, 82, 85
Lost Coast, 123–128
Lyon, Nanci Morris, 2, 27–35,
    149–153

Maggot Fly, 47, 69–70, 178
Mercer, Greg, 96, 114, 115–121
Mickey Finn, 47
Midge patterns, 12
Montana Creek, 82–83, 85
Moraine Creek, 3, 4
Muddler Minnow, 70, 78, 166

Naknek River, 5, 19, 20, 21–22,
    27, 28, 29
Nelson, Bruce, 55, 66–72
No-See-Um Lodge, 8, 9, 16

Nonvianuk Lake, 24
Nymph patterns
  Prince, 11, 12, 64, 168
  Sparkle, 50
  Stonefly, 11
  Teeny, 132, 172

Olds River, 99, 107

Parker, Jeff, 10, 12
Pasagshak River, 99
Peck's Creek, 23
Pencil Poppers, 144
Pheasant Tails, 64
Pink Dynamite, 143
Pink salmon, 102, 109–110, 113,
    138, 143
Pollywogs, Pink, 25, 49, 91, 108,
    109, 127, 131
Popsicles, 132
Prince Nymph, 11, 12, 64, 168
Prince William Sound, 112

Quartz Creek, 64

Rainbows, 4, 37–38, 62, 92
Rain forest, fishing in, 141–146
Red Hot, 172
Resurrection Bay, 97, 111, 112
Retrieval, 109
Rockfish (black sea bass),
    113–114, 117, 119–120
Rods
  deep saltwater and fly, 111–114,
    117
  types used, 15, 31, 46, 74, 107,
    131
Royal Coachman, 47
Royal Wulff, 44
Russian River and Lakes, 59–60,
    63, 64

Salmon, 4, 6–7, 8
  See also species of
  on the Kenai River, 73–80
Saltwater fishing, 111–114
  boats, selecting, 120
  skippers, selecting, 120–121
  techniques, 117–121
Sculpins, Wool Head, 10, 44
Sea Habit Bucktails, 118, 170
Sea Runner Guide Service, 141
Sheep Creek, 82–83, 85
Sims, Bill, 8
Situk River, 126
Skilak Lake, 58, 59, 61
Skuyak Island, 100
Smith, Tom, 156
Smolt, 5, 19
Sockeyes (red salmon), 4, 5, 6, 7,
  13, 19, 21, 28–29, 33, 50–51,
  55
  flies, 172, 177
  on the Kenai River, 60–63,
  73–78
Soft Pillows, 11
Sparkle Nymph, 50
Sparkle Shrimp, 143, 176
Squire, Cindi, 115, 116
Starlight Leech, 176
Steelhead, 101–102, 104–107, 126,
  138, 145
  flies, 172–173
Stimulators, 11
Stonefly Nymph, 11
String Leech, 28, 167, 175
Sturgeon River, 99–100
Susitna River and valley, 55–56,
  81–86

Tabory's Snake, 48
Talachulitna River, 83, 85
Talkeetna River, 83–84, 85, 87–93
Techno Spanker, 132
Teeny minitip, 132
Teeny Nymph, 132, 172
Thunder Creeks, 10, 166
Tippets, 15, 31, 76, 107, 131
Tongass National Forest, 136–137
Trout, 5, 7, 8, 19–20, 55, 58, 62,
  85–86
  on the Kenai River, 66–72
  patterns, 165–170
  in the Tongass, 139
Trout, Curt, 55, 67, 73–80, 169
Troutfitters' Fly Shop, 73
Tsiu River, 128, 130

Valdez Arm, 111, 112
Valentine, Chad, 56, 84, 87–93

Waller, Lani, 107
Weather, 163–164
Wet-fly swing
  across-and-down, 105–106
  sinking-tip, 105
Willie Predators, 27
Willow Creek, 82, 85
Woodruff, Luke, 95, 124, 141–146
Woolhead Sculpins, 10, 44
Woolly Buggers, 44, 47, 50, 70, 78,
  90, 91, 93, 145, 167
Worldwide Angler, 115

Yakutat, 125–128

Zebra Midges, 12